DEAR FRIEND CATALOGUE
2019–2022

DEAR FRIEND CATALOGUE
2019–2022

EDITORS
Ott Kagovere, Sandra Nuut

CONTRIBUTIONS
Else Lagerspetz, Lieven Lahaye, Justin Zhuang

DEAR FRIEND LETTERS
Alicia Ajayi, Stuart Bertolotti-Bailey, Claudia Doms, Nell Donkers, Maarin Ektermann, Rosen Eveleigh, Maryam Fanni, Saara Hannus, Eik Hermann, Paul John, Maria Juur, Ott Kagovere, Maarja Kangro, Arja Karhumaa, Kristina Ketola Bore, Nicole Killian, Rachel Kinbar, Tuomas Kortteinen, Keiu Krikmann, Kadri Laas, Else Lagerspetz, Lieven Lahaye, James Langdon, Jungmyung Lee, Kai Lobjakas, Michelle Millar Fisher, Maria Muuk, Sheere Ng, Sandra Nuut, Laura Pappa, Jack Self, Indrek Sirkel, Paul Soulellis, Triin Tamm, Laura Toots, Alice Twemlow, Loore Viires, Sean Yendrys, Justin Zhuang

DEAR FRIEND COVER VISUALS
Mai Bauvald, Pärtel Eelmere, Martina Gofman, Kersti Heile, Laura Merendi, Mikk Oja, Rex, Johanna Ruukholm, Robin Siimann

GRAPHIC DESIGN
Ott Kagovere

COPYEDITING
Rachel Kinbar

TYPEFACES
Cap Sizun by Rex
Ladna by Andree Paat (Tüpokompanii)

PAPER
Serixo 100g
Munken Polar Rough 300g

PRINTED BY
Tallinn Book Printers

SUPPORTED BY
Cultural Endowment of Estonia

TABLE OF CONTENTS

Dear Reader,

By initiating the *Dear Friend* project in 2019 at The Estonian Academy of Arts, we wished to make space for writing about the design and visual culture around us, at home and abroad. The platform that we imagined and slowly started building by publishing one letter a month is an independent publication with which we try to bring together a community of thinkers and practitioners. The letters are an honest excuse to reach out to you, the reader, and the writer that we would like to hear from.

Our community grew over the years and the project now gathers 44 letters from 39 authors, which you can browse and read on the following pages. Since 2021, the letters have had covers created by young designers. The previous cover visuals were selected or created by the writers themselves.

Some might believe publishing mail or letters on paper is anachronistic in a time when most publications have moved online. We enjoy the making of the letters on paper: the printing, folding, sticking, stamping, and posting them. To provide some more context, we invited friends and colleagues Lieven Lahaye and Else Lagerspetz to think about how they see *Dear Friend* and put it here in writing. In his essay "Stylishly fold your latest into your back pocket," artist Lieven Lahaye writes about folding and all the many folds that he has seen and experienced in art world publishing. Designer and writer Else Lagerspetz's "Carving a Spot for Oneself" digs into the world of self-publishing by comparing the publication with The Sims video game's self-publishing option and early fanzines. She also opens up the many characteristics of self-publishing. In discussion with the design writer, researcher, and also a dear friend Justin Zhuang, we talk about how the publication has evolved over the four years.

Else writes in her essay that "the driving force behind *Dear Friend* lies in connection and connecting with people." We connect slowly, intimately, via mail, on paper, and now here on the pages of this book.

Sincerely,
Sandra & Ott

A CONVERSATION BETWEEN FRIENDS

Sandra Nuut and Ott Kagovere interviewed by Justin Zhuang

Sandra and I first met in New York City when we were both studying at the School of Visual Arts' design criticism programme in 2013. I was assigned a desk next to hers and we became friends. Perhaps it was because we were two foreigners making sense of American culture. Or that we both came from tiny countries—Estonia and Singapore—lacking in critical writing about design. In any case, we started exchanging emails. At first, it was forwarding articles and links to upcoming events. Then it came accompanied with a rant. After I returned to Singapore, these grew into longer emails, annual greeting cards and copies of Dear Friend! *I still remember receiving the first issue (actually, it was the second issue because the first got lost in the mail) amongst my bills and advertising flyers. What a surprise it was to receive a new project Sandra had created with her colleague, Ott. It was a beautifully simple gesture: a one-page black-and-white letter to a friend that can be economically sent all around the world. Over the last two years, it has been a treat to hear from friends and strangers from around the world (especially during our pandemic times) and even pen a letter to them. So when Sandra and Ott invited me to interview them about the project, I didn't think twice about catching up with two dear friends.*

Justin

Hello! Can you hear me?

Sandra

Hello! How are you?

Ott

Hello!

Justin

Good, good. How long has it been since we last met? When was I in Tallinn...

Ott

Five years?

Justin

Wow, time has passed so quickly, especially with the pandemic. So, let's have a conversation about *Dear Friend*... Sandra, are you taking a screenshot of this???

Sandra

[Laughs]

[Recording in progress]

Justin

How did both of you first meet?

Sandra

It was 2017. We both started working in the Estonian Academy of Arts when the graphic design department was sort of renewed by its head, Indrek Sirkel. For me, it was quite a big change. I was working for three years in New York City at an art and design gallery called Chamber and I was organising exhibitions. I had gone to New York for my studies actually. My background is in design theory and writing and I believe I was hired by the department to increase work on this.

Ott

I'm a graphic designer and I also have a background in philosophy. Before I was hired, I had already taught a few seminars in the graphic design department. I was hired quite quickly because not many designers have this background of running seminars and writing critical essays.

Sandra

We were both new, and the team is quite small. It was very nice and warm to work here right from the beginning. It was very natural. We all came together in a way, and this department very much felt like a new family for me.

Ott

Somehow, I clicked with Sandra quite quickly because of our mutual interest in theory. As someone new, we were looking for new things to do, and among many other things, was how do we maximise our time in the department.

Justin

Is that how *Dear Friend* came about?

Sandra

There were a few different starting points. One of the things is that there is not sufficient writing about design and visual culture happening in Estonia. This discussion has never disappeared and is a constant in the background. I somehow felt it was my responsibility to do something because I have a background in design criticism. So this was some kind of a push to do something that addresses it. Another one of the big things is that I was trying to build some kind of community in this new environment I had entered and reconnect with the network overseas. That's why the project has so many writers from outside of Estonia too. We asked a letter from you out in Singapore, but we first met in New York.

Ott

For a long time, I thought it was almost random we ended up doing this together. I remember we were sitting right here [in the office of the graphic design department] and Sandra said aloud she needed a designer for this idea she wanted to do. In the department, most of us are designers and we design many flyers and brochures for the department, which can be a bit like a chore. When she asked, there was an awkward silence because our colleague Pärtel Eelmere and I were thinking who is going to take the job. After a few seconds, I was like "Yea, I can do it." So, I always thought it could have been Pärtel on the project too, but later Sandra said she specifically wanted to work with me. It also makes sense because I have an interest in writing. From there, we became equal partners in the project and not just a client-designer relationship.

Justin

Why work together on the project?

Sandra

I enjoy working in situations where it is a conversation. *Dear Friend* definitely tries to be one. For me, the project came out over different conversations. I remember very clearly that there were several lunches with Ott where I was talking about the idea. "Oh, there could be this writing thing. There could be this publication...". In the beginning, it wasn't like there was going to be a *Dear Friend*. There were these little conversations where I was trying to "touch" Ott's buttons [laughs] to see if he was interested. Nothing was really precise in the beginning.

Ott

First of all, I thought it was a great idea. We had discussed many times in the department, and in many different ways, that we needed a design reader or something. In that sense, I wanted to work on this project as well. The main thing is it's easier to do things if you have a good colleague with a good working relationship. After all, it's taking up extra work. Doing it together prevents the project from dying out because we're responsible for one another. If I forget about the project, Sandra reminds me. If you're doing the project alone, it's easier to say I don't have the time this week so I won't do it.

Justin

How did you arrive at the format of a letter distributed via snail mail? It seems rather archaic in this day of e-mails, instant messages and social media.

Sandra

It comes from a very personal experience. I receive so many emails in one day that I can't have the time for anything else. This was one of the considerations from the beginning: that we have to redirect attention. It has to be something that the person notices. It didn't seem that there was any point in doing another newsletter or online publication. It's something you have to notice outside of your other things online. We tried to visualise the simple gesture of having this little letter among your bills in the mailbox, which you either take with you in the morning to read on a tram or you come home to and have a little moment on your sofa. It's not very long. It's just one page. That's something we thought of since the beginning.

Ott

The sofa situation can also be quite pleasant if you have this big paper format. After all, reading another website or app in the evening can be tiring or boring because you've been doing it the whole day. We very specifically discussed how we wanted to do a very slow, but very persistent, communication to a chosen number of people. To this day, we've managed to release it every month. Although sometimes it's a little late.

Sandra

There are little things we can't control. Like the printer running out of ink.

Justin

Dear Friend is printed in the department?

Ott

Yes, that's also something we discussed. How to produce something that would not cost too much as a side project, and we could tap on resources around us. That's why it's one page and easy to fold all by ourselves. If we had more pages, we would have to think of a binding system.

Because we thought of it as a letter, we even put it in a plastic envelope at first. We were worried it would get wet or dirty, but we very quickly realised it's not very eco-friendly. Also, some of our readers expressed similar concerns. We realised a sticker is enough. Now we think it's cool when the letter gets dirty or has a lot of postage marks stamped on it.

Sandra

From the beginning, we had to consider how much we can do as we both work full-time. Also, how much can we ask from contributors because we're not a commercial magazine with a big budget. We don't have many of the characteristics of a magazine, although it tries to be one. It's very much like a parasite, independent project within an academic context.

It's not like we were the first to come up with the idea of a one-page magazine. When we were looking for ideas on how to do *Dear Friend*, I was reminded of *Fulcrum* by architect Jack Self. When he was a student, he did this one-page publication at the Architectural Association School of Architecture and ours is very much inspired by this breezy format with writing on one side and visuals on the other. We recently invited Jack to write a letter about *Fulcrum* and it became a way for him to say goodbye to this old project.

Ott

The format of *Dear Friend* is easy to produce, but we also thought it's not demanding on the readers too. It's just one page and we chose an A3 format so the image gets more attention as its closer to a poster or newspaper. It could be A4 size but the text would look more dense. When it's big and airy, it feels more manageable to read.

The fonts we use are by our alumni, Eva Rank and Andree Paat. A funny thing happened with the text font, Ladna Sans. Originally it came with some funny-looking glyphs like a double 's' and angular 'g' which we started using eagerly. When Andree made the font more "professional" so to speak, he removed those quirky glyphs that had become crucial for our identity. So I asked him to bring those back for us, and he kindly did.

Justin

Why does each issue of *Dear Friend* come with an accompanying visual?

Ott

The image is important because the essays are about visual culture. It makes the letters more accessible and interesting as they go out to a lot of artists and designers who can maybe relate to a visual better.

Sandra

In the beginning, the visuals were selected by the writers. They are now created by young designers. Writing can live without visuals, but since the beginning there was this idea of having a "cover" for each issue.

Justin

Tell us more about how you select your writers. What is the brief to them?

Sandra

Like any publication, we have a yearly plan where we select writers because they are connected to some design event or project. We also try to see what is happening around us and react to certain events. For example, in 2020 there were protests after the murder of George Floyd in the United States. We wanted to hear from people there and reached out to Alicia Ajayi who lives in New York. In her letter, she reflected on the effects of the events at the time.

Ott

We have also realised we are not that kind of magazine that can react very quickly to current events. We try to give our writers a lot of time ahead because the payment is small, and quite often, they are not professionals who can write something quickly.

Sandra

This plan is also rather flexible. Paul John wrote a letter for us over many months, which became very interesting because he reflected how his daily life changed with the lockdowns during the pandemic. It was written in a descriptive way that is beautiful. He also discussed what it was like to organise a grand event during this period, the Brooklyn Art Book Fair, which must have been very difficult.

The brief to writers is quite short, usually to reflect on something they are involved with. But not everyone reacts to it exactly and there can be surprises. In the beginning, it was slightly frustrating. Looking back, it's something rather nice actually that the letters may take you somewhere else unexpected.

Justin

Dear Friend touches on subjects in and around design. How do you think the letter writing format helps the writers?

Ott

This was a decision we made right from the beginning because we had almost no funding. How then do we ask someone to write for a small fee such that all of us won't feel bad? If we asked for an essay or research paper, it'll be too much work. But a personal letter is an easier task. And also because we invite many people who are not professional writers, a letter is somehow more relatable, like a blog entry or a longer Facebook post. It also provides the writer, or we like to hope so, a way to fiction. If you write to a made-up person, you can say whatever you want.

Sandra

It gives the writers some possibility to relax. The idea is you write to a friend who could be imaginary or someone specific in mind. This leads you to produce text that is less filtered and usually more honest. You might also write about something that you wouldn't otherwise write about. The format is definitely something that opens the writer in a different way.

We invited Arja Karhumaa to write about her doctoral thesis on design as writing, but the letter became an opportunity for her to share something she discovered about herself that could not be put in her thesis. She had aphantasia, a phenomenon which she can't visualise images. She found herself this opportunity to write about something personal in this letter format that somehow worked beautifully well.

Justin

What are some other highlights from the over 30 letters you received?

Sandra

Alice Twemlow's letter was also really nice. We approached her with a different brief, but she wrote back with this goodbye letter to design and it's very funny. I also like the one by Loore Viires, who is a graphic designer and runs the publishing house, Knock! Knock! Books. I really enjoyed her letter about failure and all her unfinished projects. It's brutally honest, but it's also funny. It's this interesting combination that I can't achieve in my own writing.

Ott

One thing that I like is how Rachel Kinbar, our language editor, will make these personal comments along with her edits. I remember a letter by the type designer Jungmyung Lee who wrote that she has a cat called Noodle, and Rachel commented: "I also have a cat called Noodle." It's great to find these personal comments among otherwise formal edits and grammatical corrections.

As a designer, I also really liked the letter from James Langdon who sent over a Shutterstock image for the cover that he found via Google search. We bought it in the end when we realised the image was too low-resolution, but we were so used to the watermark logos covering the image that we actually photoshopped them back to the high-res image. In his design practice, James always makes these very specific design decisions that are easily missed, but in the end make the work very interesting. In that sense photoshopping the logos back to the high-res image felt like a very "Jamesian" move.

Sandra

In a way, we think of *Dear Friend* as a small community project or at least this is how it came about, but the letters have somehow softly opened some new doors too...

Ott

For example, a few months ago we reached out to Nell Donkers in Amsterdam to write a letter because they are also doing a nice letter-based project in de Appel, *The Remote Archivist*. She liked *Dear Friend* and was very interested in having the project in their archive, and so she invited us to visit her during the museum's "Catching Up in the Archive" event. We thought we were going there just to meet her for lunch. But one day before the meeting, we saw on Instagram that it was for an official live event. It was a very funny and unexpected situation that we did not foresee.

A perk when you have this kind of a project is you have an alibi to write to people you are interested in having a conversation with. For instance, we like Paul Soulellis' work and he was on the *Dear Friend* mailing list from the start. Later, we reached out to him to write a letter, and this has led on to a longer collaboration. For instance, he will be giving a talk about his work at the Queer.Archive.Work during our upcoming *Dear Friend* exhibition.

Justin

How has *Dear Friend* grown since 2018? It seems the letter writers are no longer just your friends.

Ott

We ran out of friends to write to! [Laughs]

Sandra

It is true that the circle of writers has grown wider. The early letters were definitely from friends and colleagues because we were very shy in the beginning. We didn't have much money to pay our writers too. So it was sort of like asking for favours. But with more letters, we gained more confidence, and it is much easier to ask someone who is not a close contact now. We don't personally know some of the newer writers, but there is still some kind of connection.

Ott
In the beginning, it was also a project that nobody understood or had expectations of. But after two years, we now have a website that catalogues the letters. The seriality or persistence of publishing monthly really paid off because when you reach out to someone, it seems like an actual publication and not just a side project.

Sandra
One change is we started getting young designers to create visuals for the letters. The project has become a platform and distributed rather widely. It now goes out to over 100 different design professionals, design schools and so on. So these young designers, who are mostly our alumni, can get some kind of space to do a bit more experimental work.

Something that has never changed about the project is that each letter is given out free and we have never asked for money or compensation.

Ott
People have asked for a subscription, but quite often we decline for practical reasons. Some of them have been quite surprised we don't want to grow. It's easy to make it super big, but we want to keep it as small as possible so that it is manageable just by us. We do everything ourselves, even manually folding the letters!

Justin
How many letters are printed each month?

Sandra
In the beginning, it was 100.

Ott
At the moment, we print 200 and I think we have around 120-ish subscribers.

Sandra
Not subscribers, but people we send to! [Laughs]

Ott
People don't subscribe, we just add them to the mailing list. These include our writers, design schools and people whom we don't know but would potentially want to be in contact with. We also leave the leftover copies in school or the Lugemik bookshop so people can just pick it up.

Justin
Has anyone replied to your letters?

Sandra
At first, our friends were really happy to receive them because they did not expect them. They sent us little selfies [laughs] which was really lovely. We received less these days. One student entering our master's programme, Rita Davis, also wrote a letter in the format of *Dear Friend* before arriving from Brazil. That was more of a fan mail than a response to a letter.

Ott
But it was still a very nice letter! I also heard from a good friend Nicole Killian who teaches in Richmond. Her students used to laugh at her for checking her mailbox because who sends physical mail nowadays. When she started receiving *Dear Friend*, she would say, "You see! I get mail." [Laughs]

Sandra
There are also these nice little conversations that happen with friends whom we haven't seen for a while. One of our colleagues was very excited about your letter. He said it was nicely written and intriguing to read about this different perspective of Hong Kong than what he read about from elsewhere.

Ott
Our colleague, Margit Säde, also sent images of her son drawing on the letters. She has them lying around the living room and the letters often have a lot of white space around them, so they look a little bit like colour-it-yourself exercises.

Justin
Why are you organising a *Dear Friend* exhibition now?

Sandra
There is no big birthday or number of letters that is significant. It's more like we think it's time to get together after such a long exchange of letters. Maybe this could be a moment where we finally see each other in person. The pandemic has also made meeting in-person relevant. There are many people we would like to see and hear more about their projects, so this is a form of going deeper beyond one letter.

Ott
We've been talking about an exhibition from quite early on as the letters are very graphic. Now seems the right time too because there are enough letters to put up such a showcase.

Justin
What's next for the project?

Sandra
For now, the exhibition is what we are working on. Within it, there is also a very small-scale symposium. It will happen in September 2022 in the gallery at the Estonian Academy of Arts as the project was born here. And we are going to publish this catalogue where this interview is going to be included. I think we will reflect on what's really next after the exhibition.

Dear friend, thank you for taking the time, contributing, reading, and thinking along. We look forward catching up with you very soon!

[Recording stopped]

CARVING A SPOT FOR ONESELF

Else Lagerspetz

CLICK COMMAND AND SELF-PUBLISH

The Sims 4 is the latest in the series of social simulation video games developed by Maxis. The premise of the *The Sims* games is leading virtual characters (Sims) through their arc of life by both making major decisions for them and micromanaging their everyday. In *The Sims 4*, the player can choose to have their Sim spend time writing at a desktop computer—and once a piece is done, one has the option to "self-publish" it. This command can be given by clicking on a mailbox, and the Sim then leaves their work for the mailman to pick up. As for many others in my generation, The Sims series has been somewhat present in my life since my early teens. I felt a certain sense of delight in this new self-publishing command in the gameplay when trying out the newest edition of the franchise a few years ago—here was a feature that allowed for some degree of relatability, a glimpse of the hustle that the streamlined career paths central to the game fail to simulate. You write, you self-publish. At the same time, I was amused by the gesture—you write, you self-publish. You send off your writing, and every now and then receive a small sum of Simoleons, currency local to *The Sims* universe.

Anyone that has had anything to do with self-publishing realizes the misleading simplicity of the command. The nature of self-publishing lies in the hassle it entails—and the freedom that this hassle grants. Self-publishing specifically refers to being responsible for every aspect of the process of publication-making, from finding or creating the contents, to editing them, designing, selecting materials, calculating production costs, finding funding, printing, cutting, binding, distributing, marketing, and storing. Usually, self-publishing is the very opposite of simply sending off a piece of writing.

In that sense, *Dear Friend* is an exception: the way each of its numbers is conceived and distributed doesn't differ too much from how it's done in Willow Creek (or any other Sim municipality). The process involves a few more mailboxes (some of them virtual), layout, printing, folding and gluing, but the gesture of making the work public is just the same—the publications go into a mailbox and next thing, they're published. Just like the Sims of earlier editions would find bills in their mailboxes at a regular interval, the public of *Dear Friend* comes home to another number of the publication. However, unlike *The Sims* publisher, the publishers of *Dear Friend* do not receive infrequent-yet-steady royalties for their publications.

INTROVERTED CONNECTIONS

Despite the perhaps tasteless comparison, I find *Dear Friend*'s publishing format one of its most charming aspects—the logistics of sharing thoughts, poetics, and designs are closer to a fictional virtual universe compared to how most independent publishing functions. Contemporary artistic publishing largely stems from the histories of artists' book making and fanzine publishing, both of which carry implications of resistance—towards the gallery system, mainstream publishing, mass culture and media. One of the tasks of early fanzines was creating discussion around cultural phenomena that were lacking coverage in the mainstream press, and thereby helping to create and maintain communities and networks of individuals interested in these topics. Some of the sci-fi fanzines of the 1930s included a list of enthusiasts along with their addresses, thus allowing for new collaborations between fanzine readers, or providing the makers of yet another publication with an existing interested readership. In the 1960s when artists' publications reached previously unprecedented popularity, part of the medium's appeal to visual artists was the promise of emancipation. In the West, artists were looking for alternatives to the white cube, and art exhibited between book covers emerged around the same time as, for example, land art. In her statement given to *Art-Rite* for a collection of thoughts on artists' books by those making them, writer

Judith A. Hoffberg expresses the hope that artists would have the chance to break away from the commercial art system: "The book as an alternative to gallery and museum offerings allows a democratization of art, a decentralization of the art system, since books can be distributed through the mail, through artist-run shops, through friendships..."[1] American artist Jane Logemann writes along the same lines, "This medium gives the artist a chance to bypass a decadent and closed art distribution system."[2] And not only could the book offer independence from the art world's institutions and gatekeepers, but it also held the potential to bring art closer to the people than it had ever been before. As every copy of a publication is as much an original as the other, when given the form of a book, art could reach and be affordable for more people. The artist's book turned art from a precious object into something that could be engaged with in an immediate manner and passed on to others.

In his talk at Printed Matter's virtual art book fair in February 2021, graphic designer and educator Paul Soulellis urged listeners to keep in mind that while publishing does have huge political potential, the way artistic publishing currently works is built upon the same old structures of commerce. "The art book fair is not separate from the art market—it is an alternative extension of it that requires and depends upon the same activities like branding, marketing, and selling, even if at a different scale. Instead of infiltrating the supermarket, we've set up our own, inside a museum."[3] Similarly, scholar Annette Gilbert points out that many of independent publishing's well-known names operate very similarly to mainstream publishers, just on a smaller scale. "What we can say is truly alternative here is at best the offbeat, non-mainstream contents or design of the books, and the ambitions of these small presses; but it is decidedly not the publishing practice or business model as such."[4] Having embedded itself into a large state-funded institution, *Dear Friend* has the luxury of floating outside of the traditional structures of commerce that most independent publishers are forced to eventually conform to.

Astrid Vorstermans, director of Valiz publishing house, mentions introvertedness in conjunction with self-publishing: the self-published writings of artists, students, and designers do not necessarily aim to reflect on a wider art context but function in their author's own universe.[5] The introvertedness of *Dear Friend* lies in more than its self-publishing character and the almost diary-like writings of each author focusing on their personal work, interests or experiences. Isn't letter-writing in itself incredibly introverted? The format allows for more introspection than a typical essay, and there's an implied intimacy between the writer and the recipient—even when they don't know each other. The thought of writing and reading letters has a romantic allure to it, a hint of bygone eras.

However, similarly to many other contemporary and historical publishing practices, the driving force behind *Dear Friend* lies in connection and connecting with people. The project aims to make space for discussions not necessarily happening otherwise, to try finding like-minded theorists and practitioners, to map out a grid of people doing, thinking about, engaging with, working in the vicinity of design, and expanding that grid through the readership and each new contributor. It might be, more than anything, *Dear Friend*'s introvertedness and intimacy that succeeds in creating such webs. Receiving a letter, even if produced in an edition, evokes a feeling of confidentiality and comradery—an internationally renowned design theorist addresses me as a *dear friend*, even if artificial, there is now a literal dialogue between the two of us. Both of us now inhabit this same grid, a map of designers, writers, students and teachers, who each get to carve a spot for themselves and make themselves cosy as part of an imagined community.

WRITING IN GRIDS

Italo Calvino's story *The Castle of Crossed Destinies* functions as a grid. The book begins with a weary traveller arriving at a castle. He finds that everyone staying there has lost their ability to speak, including himself, and in order to communicate with each other, the guests start to tell about themselves by laying out tarot cards. The narrator interprets the cards as they are placed on the table before the crowd, picking up coherent stories from the sequence of the images. When the first guest has finished his story, another one stands up, to lay out his own tale in relation to the previous one.

"One episode, especially, in the knight's tale seemed to have attracted his attention, or, rather, it was one of the random pairings of cards in the second row: the Ace of Cups, placed beside The Popess. To suggest how he felt personally involved in that juxtaposition, he pushed up to the right of those two cards the figure of the King of Cups (which could have passed for a very youthful and—to tell the truth—exaggeratedly flattering portrait of him) and, on the left, continuing in a horizontal line, an Eight of Clubs."[6]

This is the pattern in which everyone introduces themselves, by intersecting their story with that of someone else, picking up a sequence in a row of cards and unfolding their own tale from that. The cards in question are printed on the margins of Calvino's book—where a King of Swords is mentioned in the text, a small black and white image of the card emerges next to the text block. After six of the stories, there is a whole page with all of the cards, laid out in a grid, in which, on closer inspection, one recognises the previously laid out narratives, intersecting, overlapping. The cards might have had differing interpretations within the stories, however, they make up a tight and neat web that can be read in multiple directions, and in which being aware of all the other tales connecting to the same elements adds a depth to each of them.

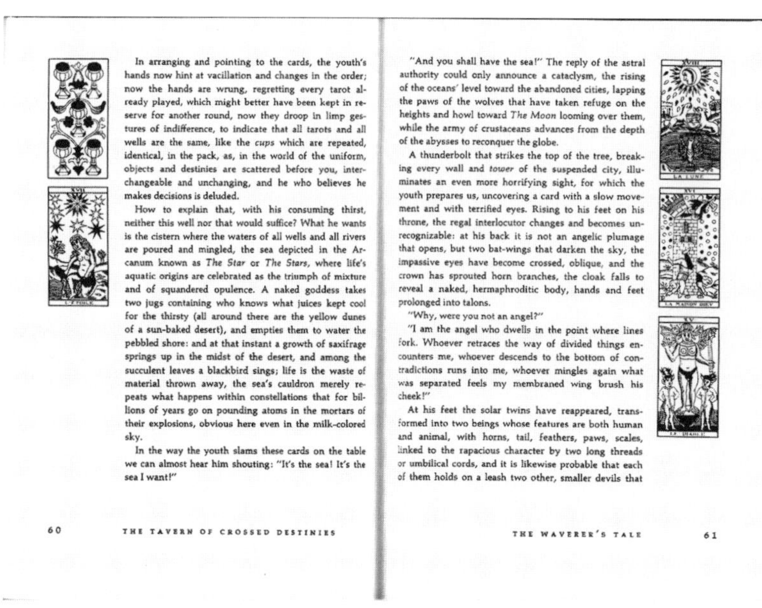

In arranging and pointing to the cards, the youth's hands now hint at vacillation and changes in the order; now the hands are wrung, regretting every tarot already played, which might better have been kept in reserve for another round, now they droop in limp gestures of indifference, to indicate that all tarots and all wells are the same, like the *cups* which are repeated, identical, in the pack, as, in the world of the uniform, objects and destinies are scattered before you, interchangeable and unchanging, and he who believes he makes decisions is deluded.

How to explain that, with his consuming thirst, neither this well nor that would suffice? What he wants is the cistern where the waters of all wells and all rivers are poured and mingled, the sea depicted in the Arcanum known as *The Star* or *The Stars*, where life's aquatic origins are celebrated as the triumph of mixture and of squandered opulence. A naked goddess takes two jugs containing who knows what juices kept cool for the thirsty (all around there are the yellow dunes of a sun-baked desert), and empties them to water the pebbled shore: and at that instant a growth of saxifrage springs up in the midst of the desert, and among the succulent leaves a blackbird sings; life is the waste of material thrown away, the sea's cauldron merely repeats what happens within constellations that for billions of years go on pounding atoms in the mortars of their explosions, obvious here even in the milk-colored sky.

In the way the youth slams these cards on the table we can almost hear him shouting: "It's the sea! It's the sea I want!"

60 THE TAVERN OF CROSSED DESTINIES

"And you shall have the sea!" The reply of the astral authority could only announce a cataclysm, the rising of the oceans' level toward the abandoned cities, lapping the paws of the wolves that have taken refuge on the heights and howl toward *The Moon* looming over them, while the army of crustaceans advances from the depth of the abysses to reconquer the globe.

A thunderbolt that strikes the top of the tree, breaking every wall and *tower* of the suspended city, illuminates an even more horrifying sight, for which the youth prepares us, uncovering a card with a slow movement and with terrified eyes. Rising to his feet on his throne, the regal interlocutor changes and becomes unrecognizable: at his back it is not an angelic plumage that opens, but two bat-wings that darken the sky, the impassive eyes have become crossed, oblique, and the crown has sprouted horn branches, the cloak falls to reveal a naked, hermaphroditic body, hands and feet prolonged into talons.

"Why, were you not an angel?"

"I am the angel who dwells in the point where lines fork. Whoever retraces the way of divided things encounters me, whoever descends to the bottom of contradictions runs into me, whoever mingles again what was separated feels my membraned wing brush his cheek!"

At his feet the solar twins have reappeared, transformed into two beings whose features are both human and animal, with horns, tail, feathers, paws, scales, linked to the rapacious character by two long threads or umbilical cords, and it is likewise probable that each of them holds on a leash two other, smaller devils that

THE WAVERER'S TALE 61

The edition of the book that I posses includes an endnote by the author in which he sheds light on the process of conceiving the book. "This book is made first of pictures—the tarot playing cards—and secondly of written words. Through the sequence of the pictures stories are told, which the written word tries to reconstruct and interpret."[7] Calvino describes the ways he worked on bringing together the narratives of *The Castle*: "I thought of constructing a kind of crossword puzzle made of tarots instead of letters, of pictographic stories instead of words."[8]

The way this writing by Calvino unfolds is linear—that is, they follow the sequence of the pages in the book— however, the underlying premise is the overlapping of multiple linearities, the notion that in order to grasp individual events in each of the stories, we need to keep in mind the sprawling of the same cards in several directions. Once learning about yet another *crossed destiny*, the reader can go back to the previous story and nod to the minor character appearing on the margin, or they can look at the cheat-sheet, the grid on page forty, and read the events backwards, so witnessing the unfolding of another set of events taking place in parallel.

THE SUN

READING IN GRIDS

Having suggested thinking about *Dear Friend* as a publication that forms its authors and readers into maps or grids, I couldn't resist thinking of the numbers of the publication as a grid not too different from Calvino's tarot cards. The mind-image is enforced by the layout of the website that lists all of the publication's numbers thus far[9]—thumbnails of the backside of each number are laid in even rows and columns, the black-and-white images starting to form accidental compositions between themselves. *Dear Friend* is a sequential publication—there is a logic to the order of the writings that is rooted in the time of each of their publishing—but they do not need to be read in any specific order. That is another charm of *Dear-Friend*-as-grid: as the amount of writings expands, new juxtapositions can be created between the different writings, imagined replies to different letters. A design theorist writes a goodbye letter to design, their lover;[10] a practitioner wishes all their failed projects well.[11] A teacher addresses their student about something left up in the air,[12] or reflects on their own growth as an educator,[13] or confesses a hope to inspire students to explore the materiality of their thoughts.[14]

"A translator is in the business of invisibility—the better you are, the less visible you become. But regardless, you are never not there. In every (international) exhibition, architecture competition, design publication, translators always lurk in the margins."[15]—"So they dropped in a word of Romanian, Swedish, Finnish, Portuguese, Greek, Korean. The word was translated and repeated, it was whirled around mouths, examined and compared. It felt like a gift, like an opaque piece of glass that fit the palm of your hand perfectly."[16]

Or—we might notice the authors of specific numbers reappearing as characters in someone else's writings, the Popess making appearances in a letter by the King of Cups. Dear Friend, from the oversaturated interface of *The Sims* to the glistening gold of the reproductions of tarot cards, this is how I view you: as a grid of text boxes, a grid of thumbnails on the website archiving previous numbers, a grid that the folding creates, a grid of non-linear reading, a grid of people across the globe, a grid of thoughts intersecting and overlapping. A grid of buildings and streets that the swarm of mailmen follow to bring us yet another number of intimate thoughts on design.

1 Walter Robinson and Edit DeAk, eds., "IDEA POLL: Statements on Artists' Books by Fifty Artists and Art Professionals Connected with the Medium," *Art-Rite*, no. 14 (Winter 1976). Reprinted in *Publishing Manifestos*, ed. Michalis Pichler (Cambridge, MA: MIT Press; Berlin: Miss Read, 2019), 59.
2 "IDEA POLL," 60.
3 Paul Soulellis, "Urgent Publishing After the Artist's Book: Making Public in Movements Towards Liberation" (lecture, Contemporary Artists' Books Conference, Printed Matter's Virtual Art Book Fair, February 27, 2021). Lecture slides and transcript available at https://soulellis.com/writing/feb2021/.
4 Annette Gilbert, "Publishing as Artistic Practice," in *Publishing as Artistic Practice*, ed. Annette Gilbert (Berlin: Sternberg Press, 2016), 16.
5 Astrid Vorstermans, "Publishing Art Writing: A Connective and Collective Labor," interview by Megan Patty and Brad Haylock, in *Art Writing in Crisis*, eds. Brad Haylock and Megan Patty (Berlin: Sternberg Press, 2021), 237.
6 Italo Calvino, *The Castle of Crossed Destinies*, trans. William Weaver (London: Vintage, 1998), 15.
7 Calvino, *The Castle of Crossed Destinies*, 123.
8 Ibid., 126.
9 Dear Friend, accessed 25.05.2022, https://gd.artun.ee/dearfriend.
10 Alice Twemlow, *Dear Friend 29*, September 2021.
11 Loore Viires, *Dear Friend 20*, November 2020.
12 Claudia Doms, *Dear Friend 36*, April 2022.
13 Sandra Nuut, *Dear Friend 33*, January 2022.
14 Eik Hermann, *Dear Friend 37*, May 2022.
15 Keiu Krikmann, *Dear Friend 11*, February 2020.
16 Tuomas Kortteinen, *Dear Friend 19*, October 2020.

STYLISHLY FOLD YOUR LATEST INTO YOUR BACK POCKET[1]

Lieven Lahaye

“That note. It’s a fake, right? You should fold it.” In the 2002 movie, ‘Catch Me if You Can’, teenage con-artist Frank Abagnale, Jr., helps a schoolmate convincingly use a phony note in order to get out of class early. He urges her to fold the note in half, as she would if her mother had given her the note to bring to school, and put it in her pocket. “If it’s real, where’s the crease?”

As part of a book’s production process, folding is what happens after printing and before binding. Though for a number of publication types, i.e. announcements, broadsides, handouts, leaflets, letters, pamphlets, zines... folding is binding or goes beyond the potential that *plain* book binding has to offer. It’s maximum efficiency from a minimum of effort.

Dear Friend is an open letter published by Ott Kagovere and Sandra Nuut. It is designed in, printed at, folded by and mailed from the Department of Graphic Design at the Estonian Academy of Arts in Tallinn. It’s a publication where the acts of inspiration, production and distribution are closely related. For this to unfold, it depends in some part on a number of sympathetic factors that are fulfilled: the publishers are gainfully employed at an institution, have mailroom privileges and are able to depend on a network of writers/designers/artists who can write a letter. This dependency has something to do with mutualism? (Soft) parasitism? Or, as Nils Norman, co-initiator of the artist’s group ‘Parasite’ (1997-1998) called it, “to piggyback [...] institutions utilising the host institutions’ infrastructure in exchange for content provision.”[2]

The folded publications we encounter, unlike the books that convincingly take up bookcase real estate, are very *in between*. They arrive in our mailbox, but we also pick them up somewhere, find them or they somehow just ‘end up’ in a stack, between books, between pages, in your pocket.

They come pre-folded or are folded by the end user. They have a tightly scored crease, made with a folding bone, on a machine, on a table. Or they’re folded using your fingers, the back of your hand, on your legs, your lap, a table, a wall, in the air.

Half Letter Press (named after the format created by folding a letter-size (215 x 279 mm) sheet of paper in half) is the publishing imprint of artists Mark Fischer and Brett Bloom. ‘Towards A Self Sustaining Publishing Model’, published in 2021, is a half letter sized publication with a frantic text by Fischer that lists a number of considerations on sustaining this publishing model.

“Figure out the cheapest and least wasteful ways to do everything.”
“Design a publication around the paper that you found for cheap.”
“Make the copies at work.”
“Hopefully the ability to print impulsively and compulsively will result in good work.”

Traditionally, newspaper front pages are divided into sections *above* and *below* the fold, with more importance being placed, both for headlines and advertisements, to what happens above the fold. In this text, however, we’re not talking about *those* folds, where ‘folding’ is used as a method to create hierarchies and separations. Instead, we fold in order to distribute, to carry. Folding it to put it in an envelope, to carry it in your pocket, into the future.

On the Museum of Modern Art’s website, I’m looking at the images of the 2017 exhibition ‘Charles White—Leonardo da Vinci’, curated by artist David Hammonds. On the website are reproductions of the artworks in the exhibition, along with photos of the pristine installation.

Charles White: ‘Black Pope (Sandwich Board Man)’, 1973, oil wash on board,
60 x 43 ⅞ in. (152,4 x 111.4 cm).

Leonardo da Vinci: ‘The drapery of a kneeling figure’, c. 1491-94, brush and black ink with white heightening on pale blue prepared paper, 8 ⅜ x 6 ¼ in. (21.3 x 15.9 cm).

A bench in the center of the space.

Delicate wall texts in the distance.

A display of handouts.

I visited the exhibition but feel no connection to these images.

The exhibition was located in the middle of a busy thoroughfare on MoMa’s 5th floor and the handout, left over from the exhibition, brings me right back.

A sheet of paper measuring 505 x 670 mm. One side displays reproductions of the artworks, they're placed haphazardly on a perfectly kitchy background depicting a starry sky. On the other side of the paper, White and da Vinci's natal charts by Vedic astrologer Chakrapani Ullal (both artists were born in the first part of April—466 years apart).

Now I'm reading their charts, just as I did when I visited the exhibition in the museum, while a theme park-sized crowd squeezed by me. I unfold it, read the unwieldy sheet, fold it back up like an accordion, read, fold, read, unfold, fold.

Shannon Ebner
STRAY
June 22 - July 29, 2017
Eva Presenhuber
39 Great Jones New York, NY.

ISBN 978-3-032-06260-3

Design: Mark Owens and Shannon Ebner
Type: Galore by Dinamo

An exhibition I didn't visit, but somehow I've ended up with a copy of the catalog. It's a 705 x 1010 mm sheet of paper with images strewn about in a grid, created by folding. A drawing of a vinyl record. Text. Captions.

I look up the installation images of the exhibition and recognize everything: a door with a sign that says 'Friends in Deed House' hanging above it and a figure knocking at said door, multiple photos of birds in flight/fall, the word PHOTOGRAPHY behind a window, a portrait, the cover of Walker Evans' *American Photographs* book, a flag, signs, tree trunks. These are images I've now lived with for some time, as I've gotten very attached to the catalog, folding and unfolding it, the creases have become grimey and the catalog of images has somehow replaced the exhibition.

"A people is always a new wave, a new fold in the social fabric; any creative work is a new way of folding adapted to new materials"[3]

Throat and Column by Claudia Pagès Rabal, Published by Centre D'Art La Panera-Sala D'art Jove, 2016. Designed by Ott Metusala, ISBN: 978-84-96855-84-7.

The publication was originally published as part of a performance and an installation. The text in the publication is printed in a myriad of directions. The publication is printed on plastic and was presented as a thick roll. Visitors could rip along the perforated line and leave with their own 500 x 880 mm plastic sheet. I guess I could have crumbled up the sheet? I've folded mine. A straight crease down the middle, a straight crease across and some additional skewed creases.

I vaguely remember Claudia telling me it was a concerted effort to print on plastic, that the usual handout from an exhibition is something we easily pick up and then later easily dispose of but when you want to get rid of plastic, it's not that easy.

"[...] it was a lot about folding. Like an exhibition handout, I normally fold it until it fits in my pocket. That plastic was not that easy. A friend used it to wrap their toothpaste and toothbrush and then read it in the hotel while cleaning their teeth."[4]

Dear Friend is riso printed on a standard A3 sheet of paper (420 mm x 297 mm), folded in half, folded again, sealed with a self adhesive label bearing the addressee's name and address, stamped in the school's mailroom and sent out around the world.

As the forms of the publications are recognizable: exhibition handout, poster, plastic sheet, mail... similarly do the texts in the publications piggyback on known forms: letters, rants, charts, catalogs, scripts.

"Dear friend,
Thank you for your very fine letter and for the suggestion that VICE VERSA compile a list of lesbian literature. The list which you very kindly sent has been included in this issue. I hope that other readers will send in additional titles of books, either fact or fiction, on this subject. [...]"[5]

'Vice Versa' was published monthly between June 1947 and February 1948 in an edition of six copies. The entire edition was produced at the typewriter: one original and five carbon copies, typed by editor Lisa Ben (anagram: lesbian) while employed as a secretary. Presumably letter sized, the pages were punched for a three-ring binder. All issues have been made available online[6].

"It is hard to believe that for every printed letter a human finger hammered it into place. Seeing a letter transports us into the idea without further inquiry into all the moments that led up to that imprint's existence. The typo consequently reminds us of the intractability of the signifier in relation to the signified and of labor in relation to management. The laboring fingers of secretaries are the hammers that strike their 'nails' into the 'wood" of paper.'[7]

"A neat format and typographical excellence are valuable assets in presenting educational ideals to the public. (I meant to type 'ideas', but perhaps ideals has relevancy too.)"[8]

Dear Friend arrives in your mailbox (or not), you open it (or not), unfold it, read it, fold it, store it, stack it, get rid of it, find a spot for it, remember it, forget it.

1 "Why not just xerox your favorite new poems from time to time and hand 'em to your friends? Or better still, why not stylishly fold your latest into your back pocket and show it to the several people who matter? How many people's taste do you trust?", by Eileen Myles in *A Secret Location on the Lower East Side*, eds. Steven Clay and Rodney Phillips (New York: Granary Books, 1998), 223.
2 https://www.dismalgarden.com/index.php?q=collaboration/parasite
3 Gilles Deleuze, *Negotiations* (New York: Columbia University Press, 1995), 157.
4 From correspondence between Claudia Pagès Rabal and Lieven Lahaye, June 2022.
5 Vice Versa: America's Gayest Magazine 1, no. 2 (July 1947) 19.
6 https://queermusicheritage.com/viceversa.html
7 Duncan Smith, *The age of oil* (New York: Slate Press, 1986), 176.
8 Vice Versa: America's Gayest Magazine 1, no. 2 (July 1947), 17.

DEAR FRIEND LETTERS
2019–2022

DEAR FRIEND 1-10
2019

SANDRA NUUT
✱✱
KRISTINA KETOLA BORE
✱✱
ELSE LAGERSPETZ
✱✱
LIEVEN LAHAYE
✱✱
JUSTIN ZHUANG
✱✱

NICOLE KILLIAN
✱✱
TRIIN TAMM
✱✱
MARIA MUUK
✱✱
KADRI LAAS
✱✱
LAURA TOOTS
✱✱
OTT KAGOVERE
✱✱

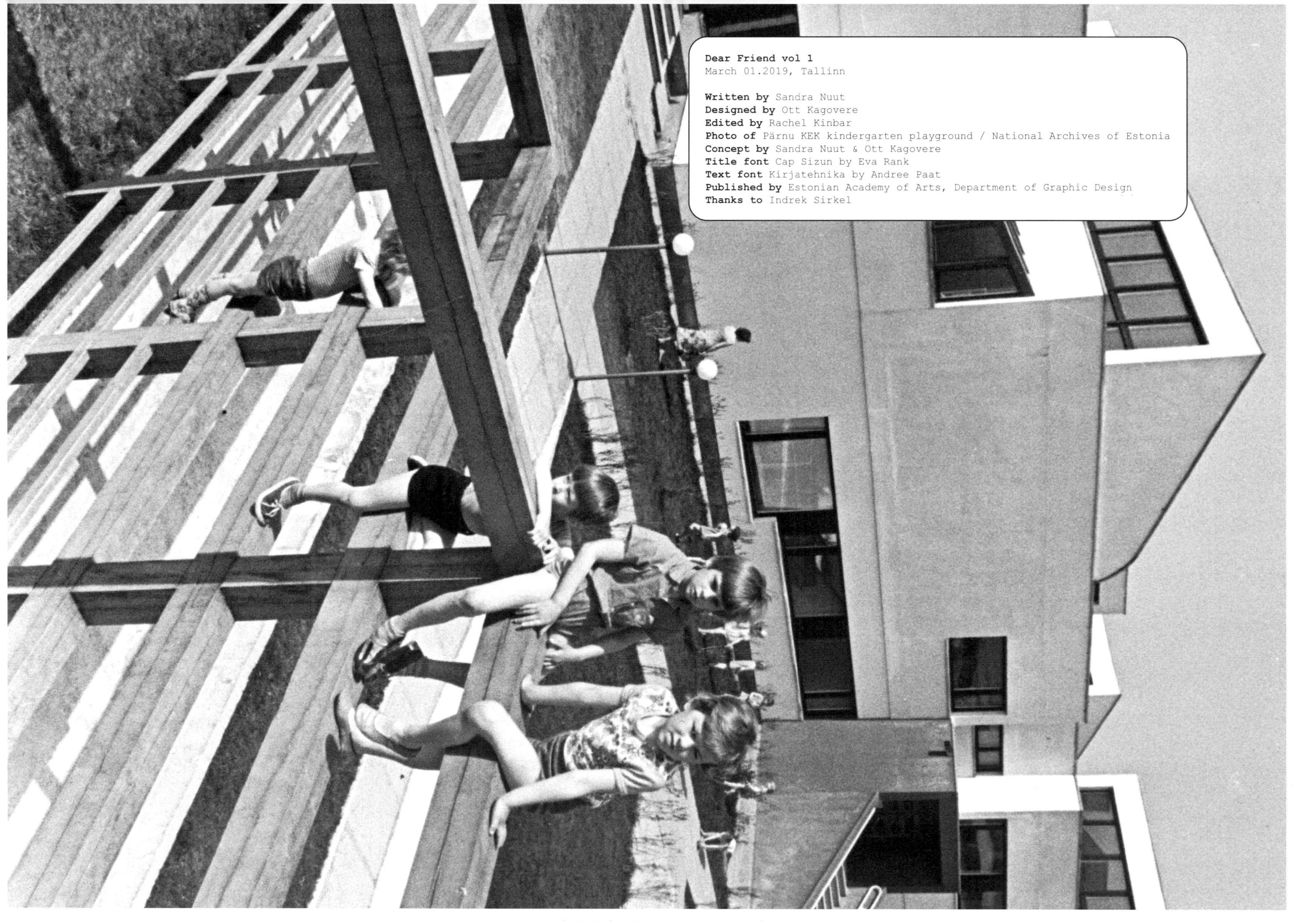

Dear Friend vol 1
March 01.2019, Tallinn

Written by Sandra Nuut
Designed by Ott Kagovere
Edited by Rachel Kinbar
Photo of Pärnu KEK kindergarten playground / National Archives of Estonia
Concept by Sandra Nuut & Ott Kagovere
Title font Cap Sizun by Eva Rank
Text font Kirjatehnika by Andree Paat
Published by Estonian Academy of Arts, Department of Graphic Design
Thanks to Indrek Sirkel

• ATTENTION • NETWORKS • RESEARCH • DESIGN HISTORY • ARCHITECTURAL BIENNALE • EXHIBITION DESIGN • PLAY •

DEAR FRIEND,

It's rather difficult to remember when there was proper daylight in Tallinn. I have been thinking of writing you, but it takes a while to gather attention, sit down, and reflect. We are currently in the middle of the fall semester assessments at EKA Graphic Design. It seems to take all energy and attention. Waking up has become terribly painful. Long days and silent evenings have become the norm.

Sitting on my sofa, I scroll through emails I missed during the day. EKA's newsletter in a fresh green uniform pops up — a reminder of a new era at the Academy with an actual building and a standardised visual identity. I turn to the advertised Open Lecture Series videos of the Department of Architecture and am thrilled to find a lecture by James Taylor-Foster, writer, architect, and curator at ArkDes. I planned on participating in his lecture, but missed it because I was in Tartu on a research trip with students. We were on a mission, an exciting project we are working on with the Estonian Museum of Applied Art and Design. Together we map graphic design in different collections all over Estonia. In Tartu, we combed through the repositories of the Estonian National Museum, collections of the Tartu Art Museum and Estonian Agricultural Museum and many others, with museum director Kai Lobjakas and professor Ivar Sakk.

I got lost in my thought. "…desperately trying to keep you awake. That's the fundamental aim of any lecture, I think," explains James. He states that the job of a curator is like being a hunter-gatherer. It is actually quite terrifying how much is out there to conceptualise and write about design in Estonia. Mini steps were taken by my students who wrote about pieces like 1930s cigarette cases, late 1920s canned food labels, or a souvenir plastic bag from the 1980s that professor Sakk himself designed as a young student for the Soviet Estonian Student Union. I remember James also speaking in September at a roundtable at the Istanbul Design Biennial that focused on the spaces of exception in education. When I heard he would be in Tallinn, I thought, wow, another opportunity to meet this charismatic thinker. Now I have him in my living room on a computer screen. It is a depressingly low-quality recording, though.

I pause James, eat one mandarin and then a second one on my old beige sofa. "I hope I have your attention…," James continues about attention shopping, attention currency that has become so commodifiable. Our alum Nathan Tulve created the AttentionBuddy, an interactive essay or smart home device designed to help people manage and understand the power of attention, as his graduation project. AttentionBuddy is a little orange triangle with wide eyes that pops up like the default Microsoft Office assistant Clippy (once upon a time), asking questions about your attention, and providing in-depth daily stats. Nathan's work was inspired by his own attention issues or the lack thereof in a social media and fast information-filled life. Nathan based his research and design around the idea that attention is a resource. James tries to see exhibitions as rooms and regimes of attention, and to find ways to present concepts that capture attention within an environment like the biennale, where no one has more than a few minutes of attention.

And suddenly we are inside the 15th Nordic Pavilion that James curated. I wonder if Estonia is Nordic. Estonia has no building in Venice on the biennial grounds. We make use of the existing. "Weak Monument", the Estonian Pavilion by Laura Linsi, Roland Reemaa, and Tadeáš Říha, at the 16th Venice Biennial, was built inside of a former Baroque church. In there, one encountered a contemporary but regular interlocking pavement on top of the marble floor. The same pavement can be found in front of my parents' house. And a large dull concrete wall rose just in front of the altar. The curators focused on the political-historical role of monuments in Estonia and elsewhere. I look at the grey installation covering the colourful ancient and see another metaphor. The rise and fall and the rise and fall… of cultures. How wonderfully distant is the Italian landscape from the Estonian?

A great addition to the low-quality recording are the neighbouring children upstairs. I suspect mixed activities, such as playing with a ball and jumping. We speculate that with the weight gain, their jumping has become noisier. There is no playground on the property of this apartment building. Nowhere to really loose this tremendous energy. My memories are sunny of my kindergarten playgrounds where we ran and played hide and seek in Pärnu — a Pärnu KEK project (built 1975–1978), with playgrounds designed by artist and designer Sirje Runge, where a landscape with different ground levels, metallic and wooden poles, pole structures, and stone walls and ceilings made up a building-like frame with sandy grounds. I never encountered anything like that later. The playground, now gone, haunts me. The stars are aligned, and I received news that the Estonian Museum of Architecture will organise an exhibition about kindergarten design.

My screen still lit. Too lazy to clean my sticky mandarin hands and press pause. James continues inside the Nordic pavilion and introduces a large-scale wooden amphitheater that filled the space between the floor and ceiling. This wooden structure let people go up and experience the building from a new standpoint inside the beams in the ceiling. The structure reminds me of Kaisa Sööt's work, who is planning the exhibition design for the art publisher Lugemik's ten-year anniversary exhibition opening late May at the Museum of Applied Art and Design. You are invited! For the exhibit and symposium, she thought of an enormous seating structure. It promises to be a festive anniversary with the many art book publishers around the world gathering this summer. My mind wanders… James is speaking about canopies that architect Sigurd Lewerentz designed. Why canopies in the north? Where is my attention? He finishes up with a thought that "exhibition is a space for attention." My attention is caught, and I press sleep.

DECEMBER 2018

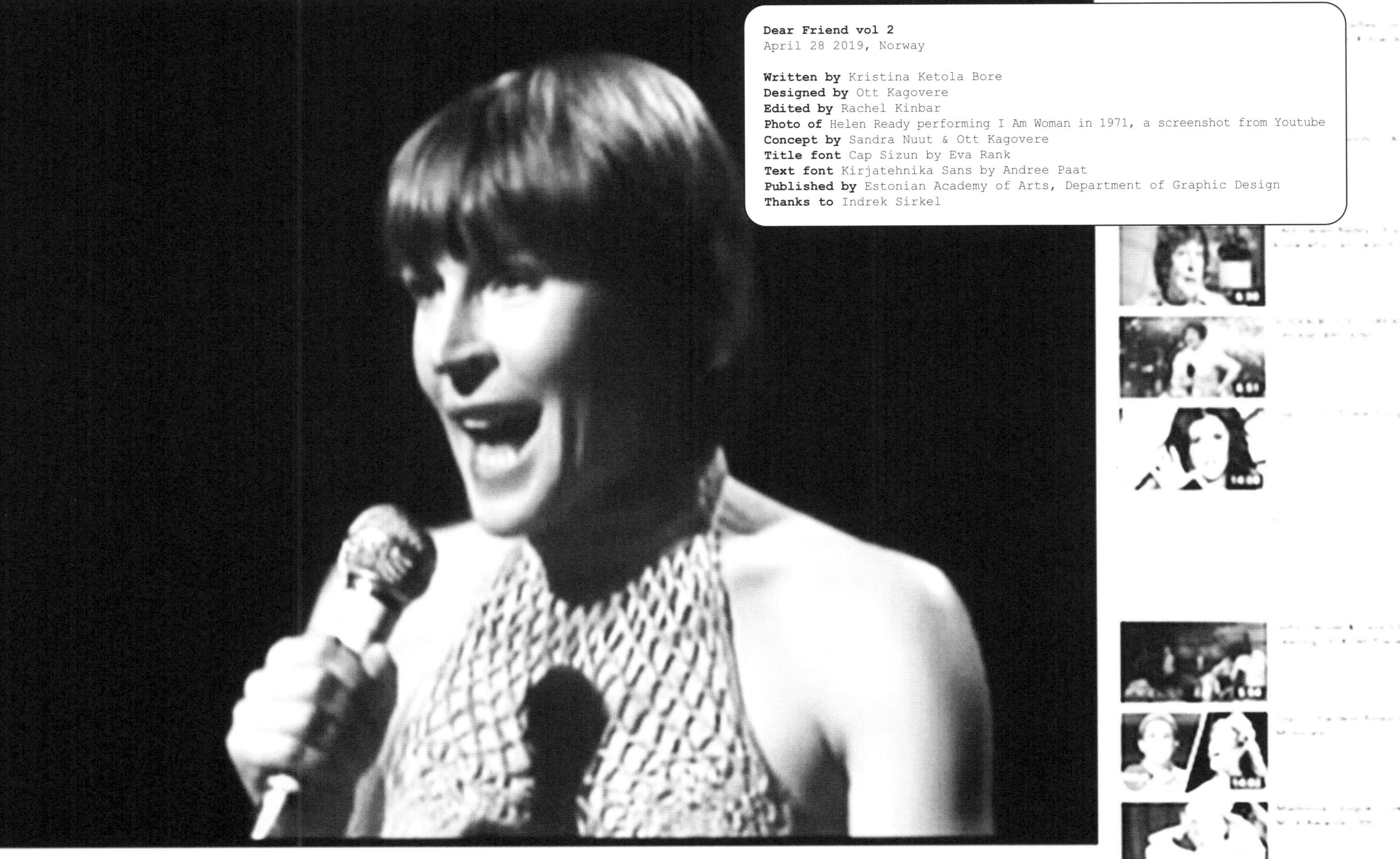

Dear Friend vol 2
April 28 2019, Norway

Written by Kristina Ketola Bore
Designed by Ott Kagovere
Edited by Rachel Kinbar
Photo of Helen Ready performing I Am Woman in 1971, a screenshot from Youtube
Concept by Sandra Nuut & Ott Kagovere
Title font Cap Sizun by Eva Rank
Text font Kirjatehnika Sans by Andree Paat
Published by Estonian Academy of Arts, Department of Graphic Design
Thanks to Indrek Sirkel

HELEN REDDY • DOLLY PARTON • OATS • JOAN DIDION

DEAR FRIEND,

How are you? Is spring springing where you are? I just moved. Did you know that? 13 years away and here I come again, in the words of Dolly Parton. I'm happy to be back. The last couple of years have been a bit exhausting – fun, but exhausting. You know, as a freelancer you can end up in this situation where you are a commodity more than your own person. And I'm not saying I felt like that all the time but for sure, *for sure,* it felt like that sometimes when I was packing my bag yet again. Yet again. I love being my own woman. But freelancing made me feel as if I was often left to the devices of someone else: the client, the student, the studio mate, the potential connection at an opening, the tax office.

Do you think being in a permanent position may actually give you more freedom to be your own person?

Lately I've been getting stuck on two sayings, I don't even know why: "Feeling my oats" and "I'm here for it". When I think about it, both of those things are about grounding. Even though feeling my oats can also be about being horny.

So yeah, it feels good to be back. People keep asking me: "How is it being back?" And then they give a telling look. Like a 'good luck trying to change stuff here'. I don't know if I'm really about changing things for other people though. Not directly, anyway, because I don't think that's how change happens. Change happens in a person, and then it can spread. Maybe I'm already feeling things change in me. But I can't tell you if it will affect other people. Also, hey, I have to say a big pet peeve is people who just keep telling themselves "truths" about who they are. Do you know the type of sentiment I'm talking about? "I am just not capable of changing. I am terrible at finishing projects. I always worry." Why do we tell ourselves these static – often negative – stories?

I was talking to our mutual friend the other day about people who resurface in your life and try to pass it off as if they just happened to have gone to the bathroom real quick. You know the kind, lol. And I remember this one person doing it to me and then just being like: "Great soaps in these bathrooms. Btw, miss you." And me saying "I would have missed me too if I didn't call me for 6 months."

So why am I talking about resurfacing? I think because anytime you do decide to go back to something or return to a place – specifically geographical locations – I think we struggle with separating the us that is now and the us that was then. Do you know that one of the theories Stephen Hawking thought was plausible was parallel universes? Which would also open for time-space being flexible components. Ok, super floaty, but what I mean is: It is not a given that we are actually moving on a linear time scale. Perhaps the timeline is indeed flexible and as I'm typing this, in a separate layer of this space-time continuum, we are hanging out. Bet we are having fun. Right?!

Anyway. Anyone who has been in any of my workshops or heard me talk about writing will most likely know I'm a little obsessed with Joan Didion. Maybe I even talked to you about her? You know, she retyped some of Ernest Hemingway's works to learn his sentence structure. Her work is so very much about rhythm, about the use of negative and positive space. I'm not giving any white dude credit for the accomplishment of women, because sure thing Didion would have aced writing no matter how she got there. Some voices just won't be silenced. However, my favorite quote by her is "We tell ourselves stories in order to live." This, of course, also makes me think about which story I'm telling myself. And maybe you're also thinking the same about yourself, since I just brought it up. Perhaps Didion at one point told herself that a truth could be found in a man's stories. Though I hope not and also I doubt it. While most womxn find their truths in themselves (let's be real, no dude will ever really know what the struggle and intense joy of being a womxn really entails) and searching too hard in men will most likely see you lose the fantastic parts that make up *you.*

I often think of this specifically when it comes to charismatic or powerful male teachers (especially those with never-ending tenure) who don't know where their power must end when it comes to female students. But not only students – often they act this way with their female colleagues as well. Did I ever tell you the story of when I was teaching in the design department at the Oslo Academy of the Arts? I developed and taught a course for four years there, and I was heading into class when I met one of the 'lifers' professors whom I had first met when I started teaching there, and who had at times helped me with photocopies of essays for students when my card didn't work (a frequent problem at the time). We got talking and he was like "Wait, you're heading in to teach a class? You teach here?" and to myself I was like "What is this guy on about?!" and he went: "I just thought you had a boyfriend here." Yeah. Wtf. This story doesn't define me or my teaching practice, but it does contribute to the long story of female abuse in all the different ways it happens in the academic structure. Stop quenching female truth, dudes!

As I'm moving out of teaching mode – had my last tutorials this week – I'm also trying to revisit the moments I have encountered in the last EIGHT (wow shizzles!) years of teaching. That went fast. I may return to it at some point, but I do think any teacher needs to ask how much teaching is about you and how much it is about the students.

When I graduated from my MA, I was already setting up to teach. My thesis was about how practitioners of design can find ways to reflect on their own field and practice. There are no easy ways, but I proposed writing is one of them. It gives you space to be with yourself at the same time as sharing ideas with others. And I truly think that's applicable to many fields in the arts. Though not everyone enjoys it. But I do guess this is my "see you later" letter to my freelance practice. I might return, but for now I am feeling new roads ahead, my oats (as per usual lol), wondering how putting down roots will affect my restlessness and pattern of always needing to move. I'm more excited than I have been in a while, though. That must be good?

Anyway. In the words of Helen Reddy: "I'm still an embryo with a long, long way to go." But I usually know how to get there.

Dear Friend vol 3
Mai 20 2019, Helsinki

Written by Else Lagerspetz
Designed by Ott Kagovere
Edited by Rachel Kinbar
Photo of Tallinn-Helsinki ferry postcards
Concept by Sandra Nuut & Ott Kagovere
Title font Cap Sizun by Eva Rank
Text font Kirjatehnika Sans by Andree Paat
Published by Estonian Academy of Arts, Department of Graphic Design
Thanks to Indrek Sirkel

331322

Built in 2008, 35,918 GT, Length 185 m,
Ice class 1 A Super, 2,500 passengers,
220 cars, 736 berths, Estonian flag

170327A

Abp/Niklas vykort ab

114

7 350320 600019

DEAR FRIEND,

The last couple of days have been very warm and sunny — one of those rare days when everyone seems to feel an urgent need to spend as much time outside as possible. I've found it hard to keep my mind on work when the forest next to my house smells of spring flowers and sun-warmed pine needles. A similar joy extends to my apartment, where most of the flat surfaces near the windows are taken up by pots. I sowed basil, rosemary, and cherry tomato seeds in late March, and received a sunflower plant from friends living nearby. (I recently read a beautiful essay in The New Yorker named Seeds, *The Gateway Drug to Gardening*, in which writer Charlotte Mendelson explains the amateur's thrill of growing things with a fiery passion — truly a piece that spoke to my soul.)

SEEDS

To some extent, I think the hooking gratification of actually seeing plants grow, and the responsibility I feel about getting up in the morning to make sure no one's soil dries out in the intense eastern sun, makes me disillusioned with my professional work. Keeping up the discipline and motivation to study while doing work gigs is difficult, man! I've never considered myself extremely ambitious anyway, but growing plants just makes me want to succumb to the dream of the ultimate petit bourgeois life of doing whatever office job just to earn enough for a steady housing situation, where I can grow plants and read fiction.

CLUTTER

Of course, I know this is not actually a scenario I'd be happy with. I do deeply enjoy the fact that I have work of many different types and media at once, although my working life often feels like a clutter of weirdly unrelated topics lying around the (metaphorical) desk and piled on top of each other, with some responsibility occasionally hidden underneath the stacks, so I forget about it. (I literally just had a scare as I realised there's an envelope from the tax office burried on my desk. I've been putting off dealing with that one for a while.)

KNOCK! KNOCK! BOOKS

The work also happens in a myriad of places. I have a desk at a shared studio space, which, however, is in a basement, so picky me often prefers daylight over the designated work spot. I have a desk in my studio apartment, which does have plenty of daylight (that's why the plants are doing fairly well there), but also a morning sun too intense to see the screen. I have appointments in Tallinn fairly often, so a great deal of work happens on whatever free surface I find in the apartment there, as well as on the ferry between the two cities. As a matter of fact, I've written a great deal of this letter to you on a ferry (however, for a while I was also eavesdropping on a Finnish lady analysing Eurovision performances for her very uninterested co-traveller — maybe this is the beautiful gesture of destiny, having me there as a secret appreciative audience as I do really enjoy Eurovision a great deal).

KEEPING THINGS ALIVE

I suppose the urge to change this clutter for something more concrete and permanent is just a basic human instinct. Performing some non-scientific, very unprofessional psychoanalysis on myself: maybe growing plants is an attempt to root myself to at least a place, if not to a profession. I do often love the excuse they give me: "Are you gonna be around [in another city] for a while?" - "Nah, have to go back home to water the plants." I'd love to get a dog to fill this purpose, but plants will have to do for now.

Maybe you know the project I have been doing with Loore — my former coursemate and close friend — for a while, Knock! Knock! Books. It's basically a make-believe publishing house, built on fiction-writing and a bunch of merch with its logo. Knock! Knock! began as a kind of escapist mind-place, one that we talked about amid stress and tiredness, while waiting for the bus after working late at school or when walking through town running errands. Over some time — and through working on the project as one of our final works for our graphic design degrees, and then later collaborating with publishers Lugemik and Colorama — Knock! Knock! grew from a nebulous fantasy into a fairly graspable thing.

Loore and I have been living in different cities for a little while now, but still collaborating every now and then, on commissions and events mostly. I think, in a way, Knock! Knock! Books has regained its initial purpose for us. It's once again less about actual physical publications and more a vague promise of something, of work that is completely ours and stress-free from start to finish. (This, to be clear, has not been true about any of the Knock! Knock! Projects. While every one of the ideas has been conceived in a chill "wouldn't-it-be-fun-to-do-this"-vibe, alarmingly often accompanied by french fries, a lot of the actual writing and designing happens as feverish late-night sessions, first fueled by beer, then by a lot of caffeine.) As we haven't had the chance to actually work on any new projects of our own for a while, Knock! Knock! Books is mostly kept alive by talking about it, either between ourselves or occasionally in a presentation format at some institution or art event. I think it's also a beautiful thing, no? To keep a fiction alive through nothing else but talking about it. The project is, after all, about things that don't actually exist.

Dear friend, how about meeting up the next time we're in the same city? The weather is nice — we could hang out at a park or something. Although, if it's not in Helsinki, then I probably won't be around for too long. I have to get home to water the plants. :-P

Dear Friend vol 4
June 20 2019, Amsterdam

Written by Lieven Lahaye
Designed by Ott Kagovere
Edited by Rachel Kinbar
Photo of digging through your bookshelves
Concept by Sandra Nuut & Ott Kagovere
Title font Cap Sizun by Eva Rank
Text font Kirjatehnika Sans by Andree Paat
Published by Estonian Academy of Arts, Department of Graphic Design
Thanks to Indrek Sirkel

DEAR FRIEND, I've been thinking about you lately because the Notre Dame was on fire. "It was horrible to watch the massive fire at Notre Dame Cathedral in Paris. Perhaps flying water tankers could be used to put it out. Must act quickly!" Did you read that? It's what Trump tweeted while the fire was raging. Advice offered, on the level of "make it bold", "make it bigger", or "do a performance".

I had to think of a note I have saved on my phone, from the time we were talking at a bar one night last December, during a book-buying trip to Berlin. The note reads: "Trump Tower: What's the hot stuff? Case study houses taschen → This is not hot! It's just heavy."

Most of the notes I have saved on my phone are unintelligible, like that. "At the oibrary i dream of oulling weeds", "what's left bricoleur", "Beefheart bush recording kid is eric drew feldman", and "It says so in the title!!!!" They're notes I take after I have just heard or read this or that. I write them down so I won't forget – though sometimes they're so abstract that I forget what they mean.

Back to that note, *your* note. "Trump Tower: What's the hot stuff? Case study houses taschen → This is not hot! It's just heavy." We were pretty drunk that night (though I think maybe you weren't?). From what I remember, you told me a story about working at a bookshop (maybe it was The Strand?) and Trump Tower would routinely call the architecture department, asking to send over some new architecture books, "the hot stuff". I don't remember at all what books they did like, but from your note, I can tell they didn't care for the Taschen edition of the *Case Study Houses* book. I guess this came up while we were talking about *S,M,L,XL*? Ever since I wrote that text about every copy of *S,M,L,XL* I've ever seen, people routinely send me that photo of *S,M,L,XL* on Trump's desk in Trump Tower. (BTW, his copy is also a Taschen edition – the type on the spine is orange.)

There was a fire at Trump Tower. Last October. "Fire at Trump Tower is out. Very confined (well built building). Firemen (and women) did a great job. THANK YOU!" The highest rated response is by Cheri Jacobus: "Someone died." It's true, Todd Brassner died. His New York Times obituary reads: "Todd Brassner, who died in a fire at Trump Tower on Saturday, loved fast cars, electric guitars, expensive watches and making long, erudite pronouncements about art and art history. He was an art dealer with health problems and a 2015 bankruptcy that listed his apartment as the location of more than $3 million worth of artwork and other collectibles, including a 1975 portrait of Mr. Brassner painted by Andy Warhol." Todd Brassner's Facebook profile is still online. His profile picture features the aforementioned Andy Warhol painting.

I've been looking at that picture again. Of Trump at his desk in Trump Tower. I can recognize *S,M,L,XL* and *Delirious New York*. I think someone told me the one on top is a Philip Johnson book? Do you know? Can you tell? I don't know what the one on the bottom is. Looks big. There are also some ring binders. When the architect Todd Reisz tweeted that picture, Twitter user Jordan replied: "a source says the books came from Herbert Muschamp." In 1999, the New York Times architecture critic Herbert Muschamp wrote a piece about Trump-as-builder, *Trump, His Gilded Taste, and Me*. At some point in the story, Trump, Johnson, and Muschamp meet at MoMa to have their portrait taken in front of Andy Warhol's *Gold Marilyn Monroe*. "There's a large sculpture in the middle of the room, a brass floor piece by Donald Judd. Evidently Mr. Trump mistakes it for a coffee table, for he uses it as one, tossing his overcoat and some binders full of pictures on top of it as we walk over to the painting."

"In late 1946 I and four other soldiers went by bus from Fort McClellan, Alabama, to Los Angeles, where we inveigled a ride from the Army Air Force to San Francisco in order to be shipped to Korea to pester the world. This was the first time that I saw the Southwest, unfortunately according to the days and nights of the bus. Since everyone knows that nothing is accidental and that everything is fully planned, it's not surprising that I sent a telegram saying: DEAR MOM VAN HORN TEXAS. 1260 POPULATION. NICE TOWN BEAUTIFUL COUNTRY MOUNTAINS – LOVE DON 1946 DEC 17 PM 5 45." [from: Donald Judd's 'Marfa, Texas' essay]

I visited Marfa once, though I didn't know who Donald Judd was at the time. Before going, I remember reading that the town was an artist's community and thinking "yeah right". Now, I'm curious to go back. I'd like to see his bookshelves. When we visited the Donald Judd house in New York, the guide told us that the books on his New York bookshelf were the last ones he ever bought. They would've been shipped off to Marfa and added to the library over there, if he hadn't passed away. Even this haphazard collection made a lot of sense.

You know, I think I also never really cared for that *Case Study Houses* book – or the entire Case Study Houses project, for that matter. The book itself is a terrible, gigantic coffee table book. I'm surprised Trump Tower wasn't interested. My favorite Case Study Houses are the ones that are now listed as "Remodeled beyond recognition".

How are the bookshelves in your shop holding up? I just remembered that I promised you I'd build a lamp for them, but maybe all you need are some flashlights that customers can use? I'm including a picture of my colleague digging through the bookshelves, using the flashlight on his phone. Maybe it's better to get some flashlights. In which case, I'd be happy to make some hooks to hang them on.

Dear Friend vol 5
July 20 2019, Singapore

Written by Justin Zhuang
Designed by Ott Kagovere
Edited by Rachel Kinbar
Photo of Viita chair by Hugo Passos at Fiskars Village in Finland and see-saw swing at Pärnu beach in Estonia
Concept by Sandra Nuut & Ott Kagovere
Title font Cap Sizun by Eva Rank
Text font Kirjatehnika Sans by Andree Paat
Published by Estonian Academy of Arts, Department of Graphic Design
Thanks to Indrek Sirkel

DEAR FRIEND, It has been two weeks since I returned to tropical Singapore. The sweltering heat outside makes me yearn for the cooler weather during my recent trip to Tallinn, Copenhagen and Helsinki. More than comfort, I find that living with the seasons makes one more sensitive to the environment. The daily need to respond to the weather — be it making plans or dressing accordingly — reminds us of how we relate to nature. But weather along the equator is significantly less drastic. In fact, I used to think we had no seasons until I attended a discussion on produce in Singapore last week. One of the chefs reminded us that different species of fish thrive in the seas around our island depending on the time of the year. But as few of us cook and shop in supermarkets selling only imported produce, we have lost such knowledge of how nature works.

PRINCIPLES

FRICTION

CREATIVE CITIES

DEATH

HUMAN

I suppose this is why we call Singapore an "air-conditioned nation". The air-conditioner is indeed ubiquitous here, offering a convenient practical solution for living comfortably in the tropics. Have you seen our newest attraction, Jewel Changi Airport? It is an air-conditioned shopping mall with a forest inside — how apt! But the connection is not just literal. Consider how the air-conditioner produces comfort by sealing up a space, such that the climate becomes forgotten. It is the perfect metaphor for how modern Singapore works.

This reminds me of how Beatriz Colomina and Mark Wigley described modern design in their 2016 book, *Are We Human?* "Good design is an anesthetic. The smooth surfaces of modern design eliminate friction, removing bodily and psychological sensation." Indeed, much of design in Singapore (and the world) is fixated on "problem solving" and ignorant of its impact on the human. As my recent credit card bill from the trip will attest, tech companies' pursuit of "seamless" experiences, often by reducing "friction" in our interactions with their products, comes at a cost. *My* cost! Tapping away through purchases, and the confusion of different currencies, I quickly lost track of my spending. So much for being "user-centred"; what they probably care about is "*consumer*-centred" design!

In contrast, I was delighted to have discovered Helsinki's new Oodi Library. The architecture and interiors are beautiful. Plus, its impressive how this library has gone beyond books, offering access to production tools and multimedia facilities. But the most impressive feature is an A4-sheet found everywhere in Oodi. On it, the library outlines four principles — equality, respect, comfort, and promise — to ensure this "shared living room" lives up the promise that "Oodi is for all of us". A simple set of parameters to create an inclusive public space. Typically, one expects rules that clearly state permissible activities and behaviour. But Oodi has left it to its users to figure out how to abide by its principles to achieve the desired outcome. Although rules remove ambiguity, the only responses are to abide or ignore them. Principles, however, offer space for different responses which can be negotiated based on different contexts. Behaviour that is acceptable to the youth may irk the elderly, but should one group prevail over the other all the time?

Creating space for such "human agency" was most striking while in Tallinn when I learnt how an ex-squat was turned into the Contemporary Art Museum of Estonia, as well as how the neighbouring Lugemik bookstore was once a garage. I am probably romanticising the efforts, but the notion of a community building something for themselves and staying independent is precious. Especially when art and design is increasingly being co-opted by governments and corporations for their own political and economic ends. Through my travels, I found myself exploring each destination's "creative city", what has become a template for organising culture for the tourist gaze. From Tallinn's Telliskivi Creative City to Design District Helsinki, and, to some extent, Copenhagen's Kødbyen, I was struck by how similar they were. Cafés serving speciality coffee. Restaurants inspired by local produce. Shops selling national design and craft goods. All located inside former industrial buildings. While artists, designers and craftsmen now have a prominent place in the city, the danger is they are increasingly detached from the everyday life of citizens. Much of the goods and services on display essentialised the cities' diverse cultures and made sense only for tourists. This was particularly so in Helsinki and Copenhagen where "Finnish design" and "Danish design" seemed dominated by the works of a handful of heritage brands and famous (dead) designers. Perhaps this was a testimony of their "timeless" designs, but can any work be truly independent of its time?

I began writing to you several days after protestors stormed Hong Kong's legislative building on 1 July. Armed with just hard hats, goggles, umbrellas, and face masks, the mostly young protestors broke down the building's steel shutters and glass windows using whatever was on the streets. It was an amazing display of creativity, although no government is going to showcase such acts in their "creative city". While it was terrifying to watch live news feeds of the protestors storming and then vandalising the building, there were glimmers of hope. I later read that the building's library was untouched and some protestors even left money in the fridge for the soda they drank.

In retrospect, the protest offers us an opportunity to rethink design amidst rising inequality. Instead of thinking "design = creation", we must consider the opposite, death, too. This means solving problems by taking things apart and removing barriers in a way that will not leave a trail of debris and despair. It also means remembering death is natural in design and considering how a product or a building changes with time and nature. Rather than creating designs that work via restrictions (aka an "air-conditioned nation"), it should be open to evolution with people and the times. Sure, such designs will be less comfortable, but sometimes, a little sweat is what will reminds us that we are human.

REGARDS, JZ

Dear Friend vol 6
August 20 2019, Richmond

Written by Nicole Killian
Designed by Ott Kagovere
Edited by Rachel Kinbar
Photo of occupational therapy
Concept by Sandra Nuut & Ott Kagovere
Title font Cap Sizun by Eva Rank
Text font Kirjatehnika Sans by Andree Paat
Published by Estonian Academy of Arts, Department of Graphic Design
Thanks to Indrek Sirkel

DEAR FRIEND,

QUEER

I'm writing you from many spaces and times — so much so that I don't understand the words "space" or "time" anymore, or where I actually belong. And what is the space that we occupy together? Does that exist? It's been such a long time since I've seen you, and since that time I've learned to really lean into my loneliness and think a lot about what it means to be autonomous. I'm not *really* writing you. Let's think of it more as a smoke signal that I doubt anyone will ever see. To tell you the truth, I've been lonely and wondering why it doesn't feel good like it has over the past few years. The last four years have been intense — I learned to rely on myself, to love what loneliness feels like, and how it can take on really different flavors over time. I learned what it means to sit with my hands and drive myself on my own. Alone. I learned how to be a solo entity and sit with the fact that I may never get the attention I want from someone else. So what does that leave me with? It leaves me with my work. I guess that's better than nothing. Or at least I keep telling myself that. I pulled the *death card* yesterday. I love when that happens.

REPETITION

My work. I know that maybe sounds a bit depressing, to say *all I have is my work*. But I promise you what I mean by that is that I am trying to do the hard work for myself. I cannot rely on anyone else to drive my practice and get me to sit down and write for a few hours. I am the power and that is mine alone. It's kind of scary, right? Motivation is a weird thing — especially when I have no will to make something or follow through on work that I have committed to completing. Early on in my practice, I said yes to everything. I gave things away for free, gladly. It was the way to be! Free! But when I say the hard work, it's not just what I produce. I am trying to take a hard look at myself. Feel all the feelings. Process. So what happens when your very educated eye turns inward to take a deeper look at yourself? I am figuring this out, my friend(?).

BODIES

My father always told me as a child to "stop and smell the roses." Just let it all soak in, I guess. Right now life is messy. I'm sick of compartmentalizing all the things I do, make, think, the people I spend time with. I've learned to put up boundaries for myself, which has been healthy, but in terms of compartmentalizing — I am totally done with that. I just want eruptions and blurring.

LONELINESS

And so here is my letter. Consider it a bouquet of me trying to figure things out. Like when a phone feels heavy.

I've been thinking a lot about language. About care and mutuality. I have more grace for others than I do for myself in times of aggression. I wrote that with a very different puppy in mind. A blonde quarterback puppy with mommy issues. I played midfield in soccer and found I was better and more interested in defending, which felt scarier because I never knew what was going to come at me really — being on the offensive was stressful and connected to scoring, but easier to do. You just sort of *go*. What happens when you stop? When you have to reckon with yourself and all that you have created and the trajectory you are on? Do you get off the track? Do you hop on another rollercoaster? I want to be both.

LEGIBILITY

Us queers have to be fully aware of our spaces. We don't have the luxury of just being. I've been wanting to use the old Photoshop plastic wrap filter on myself lately, listening to FKA twigs' "Cellophane" on repeat, as one does. I wonder if it matters that I make visible what is happening on the inside. It's a question of legibility. What happens if I am not legible? I purposely want you to work to find and understand what's subterranean about me. What if I gaussian blur myself? Can I, with intent, stuff myself into a folder — a room of one's own, if you will. This is a selfie I'll never text. It's a love letter I'll never send.

Letters, texts, text bodies, sexts. Bodies are complicated. Internally, externally, emotionally. I've been thinking about all these things a lot, maybe over the last two years more intensely, as perhaps I became aware of my body in a different way. I think intimacy comes in many different forms and we take a lot of things for granted — maybe especially those who have the liberty to not have to think or worry about bodies in space. I'm also thinking about the Glass Candy song "Feeling Without Touching" in the context of letter writing. Wondering when words are just enough (are they ever enough)?

Words allow us to be slippery. Like a continuous renaming and redefining of language in the context of desiring to be desired. Or the language of desire. And the allowance of failure, or the gaps that are produced in that failure.

Ok friend(?), I will leave you with 2018 iPhone notes because they still feel real:

Time is the same
as the time of the day when you synchronize and
you have to align like two lovers or two clocks

A book for all time

And you will tick in unison and tick side by side

Love this place and be so able to love
Be full of companionship and loyalty
Leaning towards a new batch of blood

I believe in magic yes, but I believe in a magic
that can be shaped post-divining rod.

I'm reading in bed and thinking of you, wishing
you were reading here too.

This is my way of saying I am always all ways thinking about you.

Dear Friend vol 7, September 2019, written by Triin Tamm, designed by Ott Kagovere, edited by Rachel Kinbar, photo of Harry F. Harlow's Dependency Experiment,
concept by Sandra Nuut & Ott Kagovere, title font Cap Sizun by Eva Rank, text font Kirjatehnika Sans by Andree Paat, published by Estonian Academy of Arts,
Department of Graphic Design, thanks to Indrek Sirkel

DEAR FRIEND, As always, I am very happy to hear from you! Yet to answer your question – "How are you?" – can be a little difficult these days. What do you want me to say? If I start digging into the "how", I'll never stop. So I will say: "Fine, I think, and hope that you are, too."

Your last letter blew my mind. I haven't read anything that touching and precise in such a long time, maybe even never. At the same time, there is something I would like to tell you. I very much appreciate your writing, but not the impenetrable darkness that surrounds you. I am amazed at how you can open up to me like this if you know that I can't be sure if you actually exist.

I wish I could tell you this in person, after a hug. I'm firmly convinced that when people can look each other in the eye, everything becomes more tangible. We are already living in times when "in person" is a luxury addition, something that it's not available with the average membership subscription. I am utterly bored with machines. Half of the day I keep arguing with them: they insist "I am wrong" and I insist "I am right to be wrong." It's endless; I will never get it right. There is always an update of some sort missing, out of date, out of data, out of space. Just remind me tomorrow, ok? I have always preferred mistakes to no mistakes. That's why I prefer speaking to writing. It allows me all the awkward pauses, hesitation, and possibility of compliance. Sure, in writing it can all exist as well, yet it it feels composed. It easily becomes too much, as you can always go back, change, edit it out, even delete it all at once. Perhaps the biggest hesitation exists in my mind... How can I possibly make my tongue slip in writing? Yes. No. I don't know.

When I read something that fascinates me, I can't stop thinking about the person who wrote it. To tell you the truth, the virtual disturbs me. Suddenly all the online services call me by your name because I once logged in with it. In the film *Chiamami col tuo nome* by Luca Guadagnino, calling each other by their name marks a desire to blur boundaries between the self and the other—it is the lovers' act of becoming one. But what happens when I cannot be sure that you exist and yet I am called by your name, then do I also suddenly exist a little bit less? By the way, what did you think of the film?

I do agree with you when you say that what one chooses to put outside oneself, to make public, can't and shouldn't become a magnet that a reader or a listener sucks up entirely. Any individual has the right to keep her person separate, if she wants, even her image, from the public effects of her work. Do you know of anybody who actually consistently does that? I guess the self-representation serves as some kind of a hook that is first celebrated, then liked and shared, and eventually monetised by all of us. Perhaps we are so desperately looking for proof or a trace of a body behind a text, a book, a work of art, because we are afraid to be tricked into fabrication, known also as fake news generated by algorithms and anonymous hackers. It is a question of source and trust. We are not used to listening to the unknown voice from the dark and tend to silence this ghostly agency. We tend to consider it noise, something that is rooted in the shadows and should remain there, because darkness is always darkness. We are always missing a face behind the voice; nobody likes to receive anonymous letters. We don't want to underestimate the body, because we know it's all we have. The body of likes, the body of current. But by monetising every image, every move of it, it slowly slips away from us. The author has been dead for a while, but until the machine can't feel the pain it isn't yet alive enough.

Almost every time I return home, I see my double. But who is that third who always walks beside you? Maybe the old myths about inspiration did have some truth in them: when one makes creative work, one is inhabited by others. It can be understood in a romantic sense or practical, even technological sense. For example, a shared pseudonym allows its users to recognize each other for the simple fact of sharing a name. Or internet memes that are situated at the intersection of the shared imagination that is authorless yet presented. A meme can tap into our collectively held beliefs and push them to unexpected paths and outcomes. Digital technologies seem to bring forth information and knowledge, but only through the workings of something unseen and undecidable.

But let's get back to where I started—me being disturbed by the virtual. Virtuality impinges on the present. It conditions expectations and motivates cultural production. I know you insist that one needs to look at a text as a self-sufficient body, a body which has in itself, in its makeup, all the questions and answers. That writing describes the outlines of a virtual world. But then again, can anything ever exist outside of the text? Yes. No. I don't know.

I might be naive, but I believe that in fiction one pretends much less than one does in reality. In fiction, we say and recognize things about ourselves, which, for the sake of propriety, we ignore or don't talk about in reality. Whereas virtual reality, with it's relentless technological upgrades, can be an overproduced and well-managed yet rather predictable sensory experience. But you are not predictable, and I guess what I am trying to say is that my admiration for the subjects that you deal with will not diminish, whatever your physical form.

I apologise, meanwhile, for the pointless outburst. Yet if I don't have an outburst with you, with whom would I?

FONDLY,
TRIIN TAMM

WILL YOU
STILL LOVE ME
TOMORROW?

Dear Friend vol 8, October 201[illegible], written by Maria Muuk, designed by Ott Kagovere, edited by Rachel Kinbar, photo of crushed leftover juice-making apples nourishing fallow potato field dirt, concept by Sandra Nuut & Ott Kagovere, title font Cap Sizun by Eva Rank, text font Kirjatehnika Sans by Andree Paat, published by Estonian Academy of Arts, Department of Graphic Design, thanks to Indrek Sirkel

MISSING SOUL ALERT

PENSION PLAN

VEGETATIONISM

COMPANIONSHIP

SHIT IN TRANSLATION

DEAR FRIEND,

I hope you're feeling a bit better than I am today.

My headache—a mysteriously accurate connection cable between my upper and lower brain—is telling me that something important is not quite right. This error message first appeared last winter, when I fell into a quarter-life depression. It accompanied me more or less constantly for six months, turning off only when I was baking or jogging and getting unbearably loud when I was at school, dissecting yet another problematic aspect of this doomed world at our nice yellow roundtable lined with unfortunately incompatible individuals. The first time I realised a substantial lack of headache was probably my third day here. I thought I left it behind in the city, as it meets me there like clockwork anytime I go. But now it's here. Fortunately, I know that it's just indicating some sort of cold that I caught from my mom, which allows me to spend these few valuable garden hours in bed to write you this letter.

I pulled up a huge cartful of carrots today from just two square meters of land, and then dug up half a furrow, bit by bit, to fertilise it with manure from the neighbour's cows. This shit will set and spread and give life to a lot of tiny beings and turn into their shit. Through countless digestive systems, dung is unlocked—translated—into elements that, come springtime, the strawberries will be happy to make use of. Tomorrow is apple juice pressing day. It's probably been fifteen years since I was here to see that happen.

Despite all the increasingly apparent peculiarities of living with one's grandparents, I'm glad to not live alone any more—at least for some time, until mid-October, when the garden's to-do list comes to an end. I promised myself to return with them in April—spring is the most important time to learn anything about gardening—but I have no idea if I will actually be up for the challenge again. That's the tricky thing about living according to one's headache once it's there: unreliability. The headache is a Missing Soul Alert. There's no point in doing anything if you're not wholeheartedly "at it with the soul", as Tõnu Õnnepalu points out in his latest (anti-)nomadic diary, which grandma got for herself from the village library and I unintentionally devoured. "The soul will always get going first, it's impatient; forbid or will it, it won't listen. It's wild and disobedient, dragging the body after itself. [...] Each soul has its own song that it follows. And everything else comes along, getting lost, lagging behind—but eventually, it always does."[1]

Ever since we're asked in kindergarten who we want to become, we habituate ourselves to keep going based on some sort of coherent future projection.[2] There has to be a narrative, a plan, something to move towards, right? When a plan fails, we intuitively need to make a different plan. I recently met up with a friend I hadn't seen for some time and told him about some thoughts I've been playing with to help reorient myself in the world. Getting a driver's license to commute better to the countryside, connecting electricity and water on an empty plot, building a woodshed, then a small sauna with a kitchen corner, then finally a larger house and a garden, if not a whole grain field. While talking, I realised the inevitability of a whole lot of headache in my story. Why do we need similar bound-to-fail fantasies to avoid aimlessness and depression? I jokingly suggested starting a philosophical movement with plenty of trend-potential called vegetationism. Besides following the soul, it would promote becoming free of belief in progress, internalised tendencies towards purity, grand narratives, and, of course, meat.

Yesterday, grandma went to her primary school class reunion. Class of '48, four people left. I can't really imagine a reunion happening with any of my classes. The 21st-century weakness of the feeling of being-in-something-*together* and strength of the centrifuge of everyday life will surely prevent these collective efforts from ever happening. Even you, friend. I've always thought of our friendship as one of those life-long ones that can withstand years of separation without any awkwardness. But the older we get, the larger grow the holes in our correspondence, and I wonder how much silence a relationship can bear before substantial alienation creeps in and breaks the taken-for-grantedness we've imagined for ourselves.

I've finally pushed myself through the academic anthem of life crises, Lauren Berlant's *Cruel Optimism*, which I had been attempting to read ever since February when I became "a subject who acknowledged the broken circuit of reciprocity between herself and her world but who, refusing to see that cleavage as an end as such, takes it as an opportunity to repair both herself and the world."[3] (You might get the idea of why pushing has been necessary.) Via excessive articulation, Berlant also proposes the consoling ideas of letting go of normative grand narratives, yet there remains one that she deems worthy of belief: companionship and community. The contemporary precariat has no other option for escaping the grid of cruel, unfruitful optimisms than to team up, tread the water together, calling back and catching up with each other's souls.

In fact, this was precisely the initial idea behind my "plan" to move to the countryside for good. In several small-talk situations during the past months, I've, again half-jokingly, been promoting a self-sustaining communal household in the soon-tropical Estonia as a pension plan for our under-waged, freelance generation that will most probably become a mass of impoverished *personas non grata* for whatever kind of governing systems will be left. Or, at the very least, it would lift the paralysing, soul-deterring stone of complicity off our backs a little more than when continuing our inevitably hypocritical and gestural creative class lives. Or, at the *very* least, we would just have each other. But this is a fantasy that I cannot possibly shape on my own.

Anyways. Let me know if you could come to visit! There's plenty of apples for everyone.

3. Lauren Berlant, *Cruel Optimism* (2011), Durham: Duke University Press (p. 259).

2. I wonder if that anachronistically career-oriented question is still posed to children now, and what they might answer. I'm imagining pencil-drawn interpretations of being a YouTuber or Instagram influencer. Or perhaps climate protester?

1. Tõnu Õnnepalu, *Aaker* (2019), Tallinn: Eksa (p. 371, my own rough translation).

Dear Friend vol 9, November 2019, written by Kadri Laas & Laura Toots, designed by Ott Kagovere, edited by Rachel Kinbar, photos of making of Tallinn Photomonth 2019, concept by Sandra Nuut & Ott Kagovere, title font Cap Sizun by Eva Rank, text font Kirjatehnika Sans by Andree Paat, published by Estonian Academy of Arts, Department of Graphic Design, thanks to Indrek Sirkel

ENCOUNTERS ART WORKER TODAY'S OFFICE EXCITEMENT SUBJECTIVITY OF TIME

DEAR FRIEND,

I have to admit that I have been secretly dreaming of the opportunity to write this letter. Or just to have this favourable time and occasion, in terms giving it my attention, and of course getting yours in exchange, taking a moment for structuring my thoughts and feelings as well as the delight it might bring to you. As I am writing this letter, Kadri is sitting next to me, as she has been for years now. So I will also forward her gratitude to you for taking an interest in what we have been doing all this time.

(Five incoming phone calls later)

We are writing this letter while having feedback meetings amongst our close colleagues, with whom we are about to finish the fifth edition of the very same Tallinn Photomonth contemporary art biennial you asked about. It really has been a great journey—orchestrating the complex maze of people, artworks, ideas and organisations into a coherent narrative for all the different audiences. Despite my endeavours, I might remain a little unorganised and fragmented in this letter, as I am constantly being interrupted by calls, emails and other requests coming in.

(Kadri leaves to give an exhibition tour)

That seems to be life nowadays, which you must have experienced yourself during all of your current and previous occupations. It's mad how common it is for a cultural worker to have many positions, and due to that even more disturbances.

Kadri just returned, laughing: "They wanted to know why there are no photos on the wall." Ah, the never-ending story about visitors concerned with (no) photos at Tallinn Photomonth.

After another temporary withdrawal of my attention to you, which this time was brought about myself so that I could get another unrelated idea out of my system and tell it to Kadri across the table, I can now return to the task of writing this letter and have to yet again remind myself where was I, both in my thoughts and here in words.

Yes, yes, I understand that telling you all this also fractures your reading, as you might also have different diversions going on around you at this given moment and this letter is not helping at all! But I do consider you a wise and compassionate friend who also shares the same difficulties in professional life. Maybe we will talk about it over our next dinner—the rules of distraction, who's allowed what, when and to whom.

(A couple of short team meetings later)

Having said all that and coming back to your letter after a few slices of cake and a big cup of coffee, and, of course, some more irrelevant small talk in today's office, I'm getting closer to answering your question and also feeling the feverish excitement taking over.

Opening Tallinn Photomonth in the beginning of September seems like ages ago. So much has happened in between. We have wondered how so many activities could fit into one day. Looking back, time seemed to be elastic, expanding to much longer days than 24 hours can accommodate.

The plentitude and extent of all the events in the programme (and there were so many), every single one supported by even more maneuvers to make everything happen, the opening of the biennial feels like, paradoxically though, the beginning of this week.

Indeed, now at the end of it, the 2-month-long course looks to have compressed itself into a weeklong event. The Escher-like complex and sometimes surreal situations have now, in our heads, been flattened into more simplistic images, like a dolly zoom effect has been used on our experience.

Understandably, whenever we answer to "How was it?", our answers must always be simplified versions of our experiences, again applying the same mechanism of evening out.

(After a late lunch meeting)

To be honest, it is challenging to look back and find the most important perspectives for evaluation. What and how can we measure? It seems that three international group exhibitions at Contemporary Art Museum of Estonia, Tallinn Art Hall and Kai Art Center, and 50 events later, we both have one prevailing feeling: pride. We feel proud to know all these amazing participants, to have seen these events in Tallinn and to have had so many guests coming to town. We both consider that these moments and conversations are gratifying. How often do we tell each other compliments, constructive comments and show up to events to say "great job"?

You probably know what I mean when I say it has been a very rewarding and enlightening experience. These gratifying moments help us all get through the long days. To be more specific, having an event with so many partners and opinions and decisions can help discipline one to become a better host, an improved expert, and a more compassionate colleague, considerate family member, thoughtful traveller and focused manager.

(Replying to some urgent e-mails)

I think we have also briefly mentioned that this was the second as well as the last time for the two of us to run the biennial. Kadri just commented that weirdly it's not at all sad. And I agree. We take this opportunity to ask you, if you happen to know anybody interested in being on the team for the next edition in 2021 and steering the upcoming (ad)venture?

In order to take some distance and provide ourselves with different perspectives, we have to wait for the next edition to come to life and then evaluate what the biennial has achieved and how. Then both we and the broader contemporary art field can judge the legacy we inherited and passed on and see the results of the encounters that happened at the biennial.

Dear Friend vol 10, December 2019, Written by Ott Kagovere, Designed by Ott Kagovere, Edited by Rachel Kinbar, Photo of flyer and fragments from the book *Borrowing Positions*, Concept by Sandra Nuut & Ott Kagovere, Title font Cap Sizun by Eva Rank, Text font Kirjatehnika Sans by Andree Paat, Published by Estonian Academy of Arts, Department of Graphic Design, Thanks to Indrek Sirkel

KESHAVARAZ LANGUAGE UNNATURAL LARP MA-PROGRAM

DEAR FRIEND,

I held a seminar the other week about the politics of design. We were reading an article by Mahmoud Keshavaraz, and as it often goes with academic texts, the language is rather impenetrable for the uninitiated.[1] Students were struggling, so instead of casually discussing design and politics, we had to talk about language first and discuss the form of the text, which is often taken for granted. We read without noticing much more than the message conveyed. When faced with words, concepts, and ways of writing that we are not accustomed to, we suddenly see the words themselves. Their bodies, no longer invisible, suddenly demand attention.

This made me think about the transparency of language in general—the invisibility of voice and thought and how we give it a body by writing it down. By embodying language we make it visible, but embodied text may still stay transparent, peripheral, unnoticed. Quite often we have the biggest blind-spots for the things closest to us, and what could be closer to us than our language?

Keshavaraz talks about transparency, as well. He points out that while we live in designed environments, we tend to pay it no mind. We might *look* at designed objects, but most of the time don't really *see* them. Like plants and grass, we take them for granted. Something so familiar that slips out of our vision. Our interactions with design become almost unconscious and automatic. Design settles and presents itself as natural law.

To contrast this, Keshavaraz argues that although design acts as something natural, we should always take it as unnatural. The first makes us passive. There is something deterministic about it—design is as it is and there is not much we can or should do about it. We leave it alone. Like nature, it grows by itself. The second makes us active. An artifact is something that is made and hence can be remade. It can be improved, or even destroyed if it becomes dangerous. The unnatural demands attention. It does not hide. It is not transparent and it provides us with a voice, whereas the design that is perceived as natural can be easily ignored or discouraged.

While we were discussing the language of the article, the word 'unnatural' seemed to have interesting connotations. When one encounters something unnatural, there is usually something uncanny, perhaps even weird and frightful in this encounter. Following Keshavaraz, should one evoke those frightful encounters with design on purpose?

A few months ago, my friends Kaisa Karvinen, Tommi Vasko, and I compiled and partially wrote a book on design- and architecture-centred LARPs (Live Action Role-Playing), in which around 15 people gather in character, dressed up as design-related fictional personas.[2] There is a quest, an invitation to an intergalactic design conference, which serves as a reason for all the characters to gather and a small plot, consisting of various events, workshops, and meetings. In the end, well, actually right from the start, you are left with a weird feeling. Not knowing how to act, what to think, or make of role-playing in general.

During the New York Art Book Fair last September, we launched the book together with one of the collaborators Michael Fowler and dear friend Nicole Killian. Michael and I did a reading in character and the whole thing was followed by a Q&A. One of the questions that came up was why do we, as designers, take up the role of an actor? Are we not afraid of failure, of bland amateurism? The answer is no, we welcome it.

This approach is heavily influenced by Bertolt Brecht and his estrangement effect, which was the concept of using bad, clumsy, and amateurish acting in his theatre plays to keep the audience attentive and reflective of the piece. The aim was to show the events of the plot as unnatural, as artificial. Born out of certain choices made by certain individuals, not out of a divine and deterministic natural law.

After reading Kershavaraz, it became apparent how much overlap these approaches have, and how they provide a framework for thinking about the unnatural in design and theatre, or design-theatre, in our case. For instance, following Kershavaraz's train of thought, if design is essentially unnatural, does that mean that the more unnatural a piece of design is, the better (closer to its 'essence') it is? Should designers then be responsible for pushing the boundaries of the unnatural in design, and what would that even mean? It does not necessarily mean wild and uncanny aesthetics, although it might, but rather the mere act of voicing. Voicing something that is out of the habitual. Think about any minority on the social scale. Think about what their life consists of, and our natural patterns of being fall out of perspective, revealing the traces of privilege and power that we prefer to treat with a blind eye.

And what can we take from this into design education? A question I have been thinking about a lot recently while being part of developing a new graphic design masters program here at the Estonian Academy of Arts, led by graphic designer Sean Yendrys. The program will launch in the autumn of 2020.

One of the most interesting aspects of making an MA program is the constant discussion of what design education should be. It is as if we are acting bureaucrats, who at the same time are having philosophical discussions about learning, work, responsibility, values, etc. I wonder if the unnatural and artificial have a place here, as well? These are words mostly used in a negative sense. Whereas, following Brecht and Kershavaraz, these terms have become positive, and their positivity comes from the power to activate the audience or the user. In education, the unnatural might be a way to give a voice to the student and make design visible, bring it to the centre of discussion, not leave it in the background or use it as an empty vessel for secondary problems.

Whichever the context, be it education or a designer's everyday practice, the artificiality of it should not be brushed away. It should be voiced. Its character embodied. Its transparency transcended.

PEACE! OTT KAGOVERE

1. Mahmoud Keshavaraz, 'Sketch for a Theory of Design Politics', in Markus Miessen, Zoë Ritz (eds.), *Para-Platforms: On the Spatial Politics of Right-Wing Populism*, Berlin, Sternberg, 2019.

2. Yin Aiwen, et al. *Borrowing Positions: Role-Playing Design and Architecture*, Tallinn, Lugemik, 2019.

KEIU KRIKMANN

✱✱

JUNGMYUNG LEE

✱✱

SANDRA NUUT

✱✱

JAMES LANGDON

✱✱

LAURA PAPPA

✱✱

ALICIA AJAYI

✱✱

MARIA JUUR

✱✱

PAUL JOHN

✱✱

TUOMAS KORTTEINEN

✱✱

LOORE VIRES

✱✱

OTT KAGOVERE

✱✱

Dear Friend vol 11, February 2020, written by Keiu Krikmann, designed by Ott Kagovere, edited by Rachel Kinbar, photo of More work, more selfies, concept by Sandra Nuut & Kagovere, title font Cap Sizun by Eva Rank, text font Ladna Sans by Andree Paat, published by Estonian Academy of Arts, Department of Graphic Design, thanks to Indrek Sirkel

TRANSLATING LANGUAGE LURKING DRAMA MARGINS

DEAR FRIEND,

so there you suddenly were, asking me about translating, which tbh, definitely got me feeling in more than one type of way! In the ten years I've been translating, I've rarely been asked, although, I suppose I haven't exactly offered to tell either. I think this letter might be the first time I have actually written about translating, so yeah, ok.

I came to translating somewhat unexpectedly, and I think I've realised only recently that over the years translating has become almost like a glue that bonds various parts of my life together. In addition to being a translator, I'm also a writer and curator. And the kind of translator that I have become is deeply connected to the fact that I also write about and work in art in other capacities. I mostly translate texts on art, design and architecture and, just so you know, I want to point out that these are texts that are often, but not always, short form and based on a more immediate reaction to current events, to what is happening in these fields in the present moment—so I would say, it is slightly different from translating literary works in terms of the scope and points of impact in time. Although yes, experimental fiction and poetry with close ties to art/the art world is also very much a thing and *my* thing at that, but that's maybe for the next letter.

Ever since I read "Minu auhinnad" (My Awards) by Maarja Kangro, an Estonian writer and translator, last spring, I haven't stopped thinking about this quote: "It was great to be nominated in the category of translation, it was like an award for adults. For writing, a half-wit could easily get an award, but a translator cannot be a complete idiot."[1] It might be one of my favourite quotes about translators and writers, probably because as soon as I read it, I was like, but my proverbial bitch, I'M BOTH! And yes, also because it's a pretty great self-own. So, I'm not entirely sure what it means to write about translating, but I do know that the kind of energy I try to bring into my writing doesn't necesarily have a place in translating.

A translator is in the business of invisibility—the better you are, the less visible you become. But regardless, you are never not there. In every (international) exhibition, architecture competition, design publication, translators always lurk in the margins.

In the margins, heated discussions blow up and get erased in the end, wiped off the face of the *...final.FINAL.docx*[2]; conversations about issues that often hit people the hardest—history, politics, race, class, gender, sexuality—especially when language is used carelessly, disappear without leaving a trace, to be accepted or rejected as if having always/never been there. Sometimes there are emotional dramas of a more personal kind, like that one time Comment (x) by an editor literally made me cry. Bc I mean, how else would I react in the middle of insane deadlines and countless edits going back and forth when someone actually takes the time and dedicates a whole comment to letting me know I have done a good job on something that I really worked hard on? I guess where there's a void, a little does a lot?[3]

Because there is a lack of human interaction in this type of work. I almost never see the people I work with in person; it's always e-mails, documents, file transfers, deadlines, etc. Translating absolutely is solitary work. Still, I'm hesitant to say it's lonely, because there is a different kind of intimacy present.

I see writers up close, and in my case they are sometimes artists, designers and architects. I witness their excitement, joy, disdain, neuroses, what they accidentally let slip, etc. Some of them I've gotten to know better over the years, there are some I love translating, some are (un)problematic faves, and some (whose writing) I have become to dislike strongly. I can see the writer as they are in that moment, and maybe in some ways even clearer than the reader does (bc of what gets edited). However, in the process of translating, editing and mediating between translator, editor, client and writer (btw, the latter two are different people more often than not), I often remain invisible to writers. I exist in an abstract way, as A Translator, Some Translator, and it's not rare (and this is where it gets a little weird) that the writers are people I know and who know me in a different professional context. Do you know the feeling when you have an intense dream about someone you don't really know very well and that makes you look at them a little differently the next time you see them? Yeah, it can be a little like that. And it's... it's a mood for sure.

So yes, translating is intense mentally, emotionally, but also physically if you forget or can't take care of your body properly. Combined with other jobs, it can be a challenge—switching between the mental registries required for different types of work is exhausting—and as a personal plot twist, it turns out I translate best very early in the morning and write best very late in the night, which does not make for a good routine. I recently went to a talk where two translators, women around my mom's age who have been translating way longer than I, described how they have always translated alongside other jobs they have had, through family vacations, early mornings and late nights—it's never been their sole occupation. The same was confirmed by a survey I saw somewhere, 9 out of 10 had other jobs. And that comes with another set of challenges (see: precarity). Despite/ because of that, it finds, or I deliberately try to find ways to fill every possible crack with translating whenever I can. As a freelancer you don't really say no to a job, so translating has become a glue that holds my life together also in a very material sense.

But I've realised that translating also carries me in other ways. For example, to say translating has made me a better writer is not exactly true—it is through translating that I have become a writer at all. So lately, I've been exploring how to bring what translating has given me to other areas in my work, to see what happens. It takes time but I'm sure something will come of it. I'll let you know!

Anyway, thanks again for asking!

1. No, the book has not been translated and no, I don't know what page this is from.

2. That's a lie though, no decent translator/editor/project manager would let file names get so messy; that's what writers do.

3. Fyi on the other end of the emotional spectrum for me and I suspect a lot of other translators, is not tears of sadness, but a deep earth-shattering shame over mistakes that have slipped into the world and can no longer be undone.

Dear Friend vol 12, March 2020, written by Jungmyung Lee, designed by Ott Kagovere, edited by Rachel Kinbar, the image is captured from "Once Upon a Time in Hollywood", concept by Sandra Nuut & Ott Kagovere, title font Cap Sizun by Eva Rank, text font Ladna Sans by Andree Paat, Impact Nieuw & Birch by Jung-Lee Type Foundry, published by Estonian Academy of Arts, Department of Graphic Design, thanks to Indrek Sirkel. gd.artun.ee/dearfriend

INSOMNIA INSTAGRAM DOUGHNUT WHEEL OF EMOTIONS REAL-TIME REALIST DIGESTIVE TRACT

DEAR FRIEND,

It's another sleepless night. Already for a couple of months I've been grappling with insomnia. I am a woken zombie next to my partner who can lay his body on this certain fixture we learned to call a bed and rest his head on a soft stuffed rectangular of foam for two seconds, at which point he suddenly shifts into sleep mode. It feels weird how the two opposite states of our bodies co-exist in a 140cm width space with the same purpose. I get anxious as soon as my awake time hits longer than an hour. I then often open Instagram (IG) looking for some form of entertainment.

I secretly have five active IG accounts. Actually, I used to have one more, but adding more than five is not allowed, so I abandoned one. I no longer remember what it was... Imagine! What if that thrown account wanted to lie glued, to sleep and wake up with the other five bedmates.

IG... what is it! All you want is to fall into sleep, but your thumb ritually taps the app to open. Going online is such an intrinsically solitary act and yet, ironically, it involves a social engagement at large. Can it work as a lullaby? Am I already dreaming? Or do I need a reality check in my pre-sleep state? Actually, it kicks me out of sleep mode. Bountiful posts and content personalised according to my growing interests, age, gender, and location might not sound so bad until you realise that you need to flush out all the Kardashians first. I am in a bubble. We all do the same things, like the same things, turn our backs on the same things. We advertise our day, promote what we do, show off what we own. Are we humans or advertisements?

I was never a cat person, but since we got our cat Noodle—a gremlin-like investigator with wide impish eyes and huge batwing ears—I am learning about cats. Noodle, just like all other cats, likes to eat indoor palm plants. Cats eat grass as a natural laxative to ease stomach pain. When I think of myself wanting to chug a couple more beers when I am already drunk enough, it seems like a pretty smart move. The other day I found my cat's faeces interesting. It was the shape of a doughnut! Its beginning and end were literally connected by a thin palm leaf.

Here, I have a question for you: What's the simplest geometric shape of the human body?

It's a doughnut! I recall being shocked when I came across an article ten years ago talking about human topology. Basically, the human body is a lump with a hole running all the way through the middle, like a doughnut. This means that the inside of your gastrointestinal tract is *outside* your body. Again, anything *inside* the gut is *outside* the body. Undigested food has never been *inside* the body. Your colonic bacteria live *outside* your body. How uncannily convoluted! Since then, none of these formulae—"inside-outside", "yes-no" or "right-wrong"—have worked for me. I believe that there is always an inter-related connection between these two opposing sides.

Nothing! Nothing shows me its honest self! Even mirrors give me illusional reflections. Why does it make me slimmer? A completely flat mirror should show an image of exactly the same shape and size as the actual object. So why do a lot of mirrors offer something a little way from the truth? IG's handful of face filters are warping the way we see our faces, as well. The huge and prevalent trend of us obsessively augmenting our realities is visual proof that we are collectively in denial. I know I sound quite dramatic. These are the thoughts running through my mind while fighting insomnia.

A couple of days before Noodle's doughnut poop, I had a dream that I was playing with doughnuts like a little kid. Spinning a doughnut on my index finger, smashing a stack of them, connecting two with a straw to make glasses. It was all fun. Strawberry caramel glaze was slowly dripping and covered the inner rings... all of a sudden I was looking at the world through rose-coloured glasses. Wait! Offering us rose-coloured glasses covered in glossy glaze... that might be it. IG's initial intention!

Finally, I am sending you a description of "Real-Time Realist No.2" and my contribution to it:

Published by J-LTF Press, "Real-Time Realist" is an experimental journal on the wide range of human affect (emotions) through typography, art, and contemporary writing, based on psychologist Robert Plutchik's *Wheel of Emotions*. This issue—with guest editor Lieven Lahaye—explores Ecstasy, Joy, Serenity, and Love, *The Yellow Wheel*, with contributions from the invited artists distilling the aforesaid emotions.

"Real-Time Realist" is a container for experiments with typographic research and the intimate relations between writing, typography, and visual art. It is as a unique type specimen, not only showcasing typefaces produced by Jung-Lee Type Foundry (J-LTF), but also exploring the role of typography in linguistic materials. J-LTF manifests that typefaces reach readers through their own emotions and sentiments. In that sense, each typeface acknowledges the role of itself as well as the other typefaces and how they interact with texts.

My typographic research for this issue is from a feminist perspective and traces back to the printing press period in the 18th century: woodcut letters, female engraving labourers working freelance out of their homes, the emotions that were locked in letters on the surfaces of woodblocks, and an analogy between handwriting and engraving letters, which ultimately resulted in a typeface now known as Birch.

Maybe the third issue of "Real-Time Realist" could be about either the Red (anger) or Pink (disgust) or Purple (sadness) sector—darker emotions than in the previous issues. Which doughnut colour would you choose?

P.S. If a book is identical to a doughnut, what do you think is its digestive tract?

Dear Friend vol 13, April 2020, written by Sandra Nuut, designed by Ott Kagovere, edited by Rachel Kinbar, image "Flux Tribalism" by Robin Siimann, concept by Sandra Nuut & Ott Kagovere, title font Cap Sizun by Eva Rank, text font Ladna Sans by Andree Paat (Kirjatehnika), published by Estonian Academy of Arts, Department of Graphic Design, thanks to Indrek Sirkel and Pärtel Eelmere

WASH YOUR HANDS

COVID-19

TOUCH

TACT

GUIDELINES

DEAR FRIEND,

I recommend washing your hands after reading this. It sounds like I am sharing a filthy story. Perhaps I am? I tried to avoid writing about the COVID-19 pandemic, but here I am talking about it—like you, your friends and friends of friends and the whole world. There seem to be guidelines coming in on how to be and behave from family members to government officials. We now live by rules that have been in place for little more than a month.

It is fascinating how quickly change happens and manifests. Do you remember the time when you did not notice people on the streets walking past you? These days I cannot walk down the street without distantiating myself from every single human being, jumping to the lawn or behind my partner. 9/11 made us change the rules at airports and in the air. Now we change the order on ground level. We distantiate, wear masks, gloves and place sanitisers at the entrance of public buildings.

Speaking of being in the air, in the beginning of March I was on my way home, transferring through Frankfurt airport. There were no hand sanitisers in the airport, nor did we see anyone selling masks. This did not keep people from covering their faces. People walked the corridors while sanitising their hands, and so did we. Some hid in toilet cabins to cough or sneeze like criminals. Change in behaviour was happening all around us. After the trip, I did not know how to react or continue other than actively read the Health Board news. I also wonder how to make or take any guidelines when even doctors say that they are not entirely sure what we are dealing with.

Although we do not know what we are dealing with yet, at home we might have time for theor etical observations. In a conference call on Zoom, an interview we conducted with curator Corina Apostol and graphic designer Maryam Fanni, along with Kulla Laas and Madis Luik at the Estonian Academy of Arts, we discussed art and design education, distance learning and exhibiting in the time of pandemic. Even though everyone is amazed by what the cultural institutions are putting out now, e.g. Tallinn Art Hall's virtual exhibitions, we also agreed that the internet, contrary to popular opinion, is not democratic nor accessible to all. While we seem to have entered a new global internet era, there is also talk about a moment of restart, change and "a blank page for a new beginning". In another discussion that I listened to via Zoom between architect, curator and editor Joseph Grima and design curator Jan Boelen, organised by Dirty Furniture magazine, they raised questions about how we should approach a time like this when governments have a lot of power, what kind of democracies we can build, as well as what we can leave behind.

Daily we catch the press conference dedicated to the pandemic, and weekly we receive news on the local far-right party making gross decisions for the prime minister. One more essential event that takes place weekly now is grocery shopping. Our reasoning is that we are healthy, need to walk, and we do not have a car for grander shopping. Making someone else do our shopping at this point would mean putting someone else in danger. Entering the grocery store, however, has become a painful and stressful experience because there is always someone who cannot wait behind you. These enigmatic characters jump around to quickly grab a bag of sour cream or take a carton of juice just when you are reaching for it.

Indeed, it is time for reflection and for criticism as the ruling entities all over the world take advantage. I am happy to see that in some industrial cities the air quality has improved, or so I have read. But I am progressively more anxious of being led by the ill-informed. And I am nervous in my very comfortable position where I am at home still with a job writing this letter in my warm living room turned office space. One moment it feels like I am grabbing that carton of juice in my regular supermarket in solitude, and the next moment I hear that someone other than the Prime Minister has laid off the third Minister of Foreign Trade and Information Technology in the timeframe of a year. My presumed solitude at the store is disturbed by a stranger diffidently touching my freaking arm. The juice spills on the floor.

Do you remember Poland closing its borders a few weeks ago? The trucks waited for days in line close to the Polish border, then after crossing and driving, they were taken off the roads by police. Fines were written out to drivers for exceeding their working hours, the hours that this one state had irresponsibly created within the union. Here, we receive unsettling news about sending home foreign workers with soon expiring visas. Again, I get a shudder of fright similar to when a person is standing way too close in the fruits and vegetables section. If there is anything we really need to act on, it is a reform of communication. Perhaps only a revolution can set the proper stage for a change in governing and manners? It is painful to think of the organisations in which people are made to work in unsafe conditions when it is unnecessary or to watch higher education institutions and museums lay off or furlough their workforce. The top keeps harming the most vulnerable and lowest paid demographics in the system. Nothing changes, only fragilities and insensitivities are brought to the surface.

What are the communal and political guidelines for this time? How often do we miss a decision that should be protested? Very conveniently we cannot raise our voices, or if someone does then there is the lack of personal contact that seems to be relevant for any truly uncomfortable confrontation (and that also might provide one with the novel coronavirus).

STAY SAFE &
ALERT, SANDRA

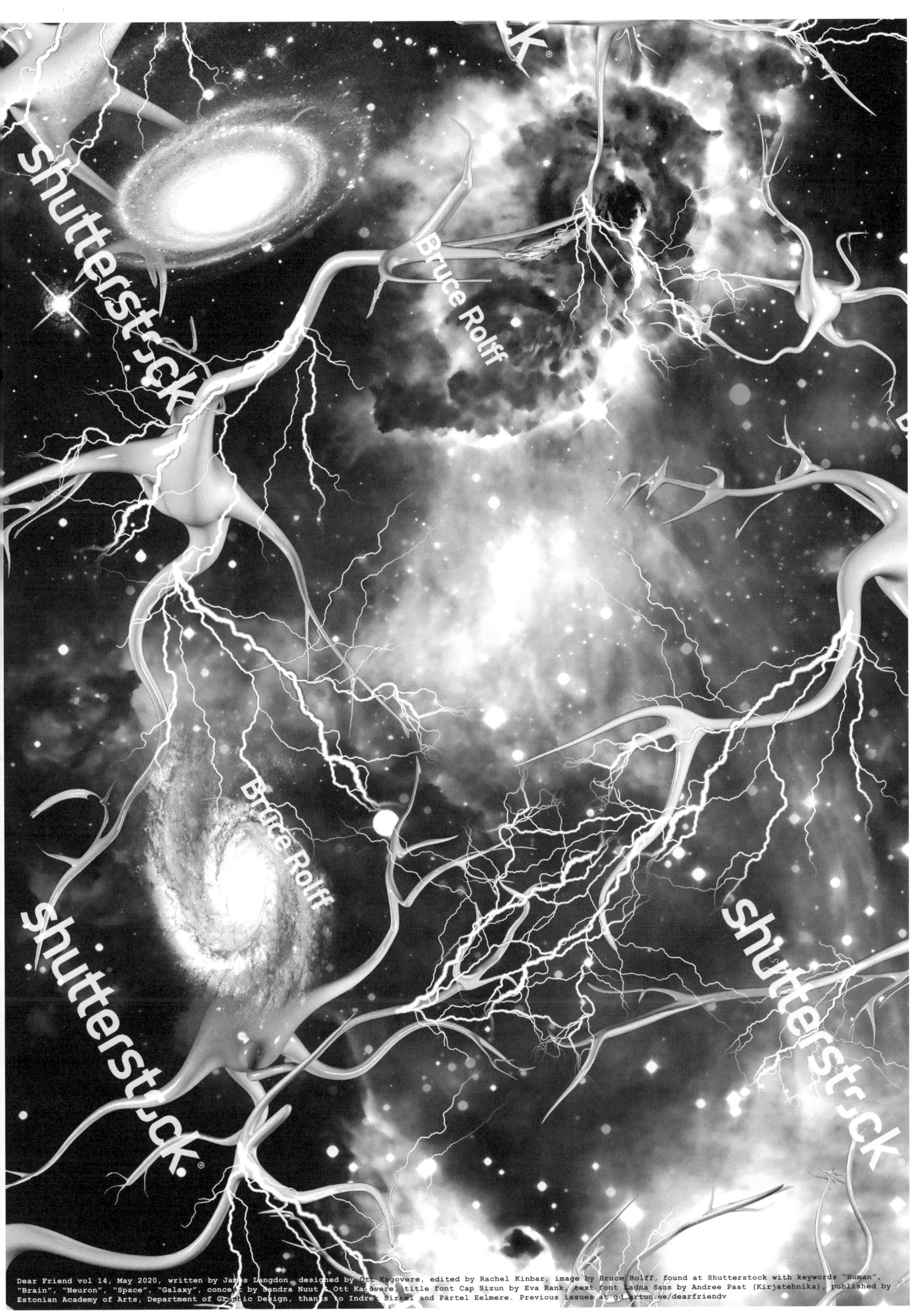

Dear Friend vol 14, May 2020, written by James Langdon, designed by Ott Kagovere, edited by Rachel Kinbar, image by Bruce Rolff, found at Shutterstock with keywords "Human", "Brain", "Neuron", "Space", "Galaxy", concept by Sandra Nuut & Ott Kagovere, title font Cap Sizun by Eva Rank, text font Ladna Sans by Andree Paat (Kirjatehnika), published by Estonian Academy of Arts, Department of Graphic Design, thanks to Indrek Sirkel and Pärtel Eelmere. Previous issues at gd.artun.ee/dearfriendv

"HUMAN" "BRAIN" "NEURON" "SPACE" "GALAXY"

DEAR FRIEND,

I'm writing to explain myself. That was me in the audience of your lecture at the big neuroscience conference last weekend. No doubt you noticed me. I did seem to stand out. I've never felt self-conscious dressed casually in black before! Perhaps you also noticed that your presentation took me on something of a wild ride.

I came to the conference feeling dangerous. An infiltrator from another aesthetic universe. I intended a discrete entrance. I would bide my time, make my move in the Q&A. Things certainly began as expected—as if you were completely unaware that graphic design, my profession, even exists! I almost lost my composure at the very first slide. Was that your own laboratory's logo, lurking awkwardly in the corner? You must have dragged a tiny GIF file from some ancient university web page directly into your PowerPoint presentation, enlarged it without constraining proportions, and then just left it there, mangled and blurred. I glanced around the audience, expecting looks of professional alarm, but nothing. I half-raised my hand. I've spent 15 years explaining vector graphics to my clients, so I'm more than qualified, but... *Be patient*, I told myself. I was there to bring expertise and insight. I couldn't afford to come across as pedantic.

I settled in. At that point I had no reason to doubt myself. I tried to see the funny side. Indeed, I found your slides reassuringly calamitous. Single slides containing hundreds of bullet-pointed words. Tired stereotypes from the first page of a Google Images search for 'science cartoon'. Technical charts shoved on top of generic, pseudo-high-tech brains from Shutterstock, still with their digital watermarks. Right-click, Save Image to Desktop, am I right? Every lab, it seems, has an amateur Photoshop artist.

When the moment for questions finally came, a polite hesitation on my part allowed a young woman to make a lengthy inquiry about some technical detail of your presentation. No wonder she's confused, I thought. Your answer apparently required showing one of your animations again. So you clicked back to the slide, but the animation wasn't triggered. I was about to point out that you would need to click forward from the preceding slide for it to play. But what you did next took me aback. You rolled your eyes, and, without hesitation, hit the escape key on your laptop to switch out of fullscreen mode, navigated directly to the slide, and then used two three-fingered keyboard shortcuts in rapid succession to ungroup the elements and open the animation in another application with more precise playback controls! Witnessing your virtuosity with the software, it struck me. This was no calamity. The amateurism of your slides was a ruse. A nuanced visual proposition was being made in that hall, and I was the only one not attuned to it. I felt foolish.

Unfortunately for me, that wasn't the end of the ride. Since the conference, I can't stop thinking about you. I had come to tell you that, without graphic design, no one can take you seriously. Instead, you showed me that for a scientist, graphic design is a liability. Graphic design *reduces* credibility. Had you presented professional, well-designed slides, it would have raised suspicions. Your colleagues would have asked: *What is this? Who is she trying to persuade?* And so—I'm speculating here—your stumbling visual language of lowest-common-denominator digital bricolage is perfectly measured for its audience. That's it, isn't it? How did I misread you so badly? I thought it was a plea for help. But to your colleagues, the message is well understood. You signal to them that you have not compromised data for 'pretty pictures'. That you are working on the mysteries of the human brain and don't have time to consider the consistent use of colour, the relative scale of elements in your slide layouts, or their typographic hierarchy.

As you might imagine, these revelations have been unnerving. Or they were, until what follows occurred to me. A premonition, one could say. Perhaps I will yet have the opportunity to save you!

It may not be apparent yet, in academia, but the tools of the digital bricoleur are changing. Actually, things will be getting easier and more convenient for you. I expect you'll welcome it. At least at first. You won't ever have to troubleshoot your presentations again, that's for sure. Your IT department will install new presentation software with an online-only interface. Much simpler. Mandatory templates will take care of layout, stop you from placing too much text on a slide, and make sure none of those crude graphics-done-in-the-lab-on-the-day-before-the-conference find their way into a presentation. You won't miss them though, because you'll have Neurostock. It'll be called something definitive like that. Shutterstock, but only for neuroscience. They'll probably even sponsor your institution. You'll have all the gorgeous high resolution images you want, and no watermarks!

Are you seeing them yet? The warning signs? To be clear, this is not about you personally. I'm sure you'll do great. But that innocent, undesigned aesthetic that you and your colleagues have been cultivating? I'm sorry to have to tell you this: it's about to be digitally gentrified.

Perhaps you're laughing at the idea that your IT department could orchestrate such a conspiracy. But that's what it is. Just look online. Look at the website of the leading domestic air purifier on the market. Or your favourite coffee roaster who claims to pay their farmers fairly. Don't they look brilliant! Really super, super nice. Well, wake up, professor! That's the contemporary visual language of authority acting on you. It wants to sublimate you with its clean templates and elegant typefaces. I know what you're thinking. But your indifference is powerless against it. If you don't care for its templates, it will win you over by automating those seamless looping animations that you like. That would save you time, no? It doesn't matter, anyway. If the people in IT like it, you're getting it. Before you know it, your presentations will be... well, *convincing*. From there you'll only be one Neurostock image away from *persuasive*. Then what will be left of your scientific credibility?

Dear Friend vol 15, June 2020, written by Laura Pappa, designed by Ott Kagovere, edited by Rachel Kinbar, image "Summer office" by Laura Pappa, concept by Sandra Nuut & Ott Kagovere, title font Cap Sizun by Eva Rank, text font Ladna Sans by Andree Paat (Kirjatehnika), published by Estonian Academy of Arts, Department of Graphic Design, thanks to Indrek Sirkel and Pärtel Eelmere. Previous issues at gd.artun.ee/dearfriend

✱✱ DEAR FRIEND,

Hope you're well. I'm writing this letter to you on Saturday, 20 June, just ahead of Midsummer's Eve, hoping it will reach you sometime before September.

Having spent the majority of my existence these past months behind the computer, I've grown increasingly fed up with the internet. I long for everything tangible, and so I've thought a lot about snail mail recently. Emails bore me. So it was to my great surprise when, two days ago, I received an email from my once-almost-friend and passionate trickster from the States, Alan Abel—an avid letter-writer and snail mail fan himself. The subject of the email was also 'Alan Abel'. To my great sadness, Alan is no more for already a while now (though more than present in spirit) and so the expectation regarding the email was fairly low. This is what it read:

> *Laura*
> *https://bit.ly/3fRRlMh*
> *Alan*

Google announced swipe gesture controls are coming to Gmail iOS starting today, and should be available to all iOS Gmail users soon. Though the update doesn't add any new commands to Gmail, it makes it much easier to quickly manage your inbox by letting users customize what left or right "swipe" actions do.

It's hard to mess up, even when you mess up. Your eggs are overcooked and rumpled? Flop them out of the pan onto a waiting mound of the rice mixture, like a shameful blanket. This will still taste good. Your egg disk is pale and under cooked? Add the rice, fold it in half, turn the light down low, and cover the pan with a lid for a minute or two. The gentle heat will steam the egg until set. This too will taste good.

ttxcr oikophobia sporing upgathered zwpastoralized terrifyingly marshy mammas[1]

You have to apologise for I'm really making up this letter to you as we go along, and so I only discovered the last part of Alan's letter this very moment. *It's hard to mess up, even when you mess up. Your eggs are overcooked and rumpled? Like a shameful blanket. ttxcr oikophobia sporing upgathered. zwpastoralized terrifyingly marshy mammas.* Good golly! This DOES sound like the Alan I know. Mr. Confusion Cooker, Mr. Hoaxer Extraordinaire (as the New York Times once called him). I'm filled with excitement and sadness. I met Alan only once several years ago at the Goethe Institute in Amsterdam where he was about to give a talk about his long-lived practice as a prankster, a film-maker, an author and publisher and an all round fun-maker. I miss there not being more Alans in the world and around me. He sent me many a snail mail, and I once smuggled some Cuban cigars to his home in Connecticut (by the way, I do find it appropriate that he lived in Connect-icut—Mr. Avid Connector—and equally appropriate that he was born in Zanesville). I do regret not sending him more cigars before his passing, as he asked on several occasions... I hope he'll forgive me, and I hope wherever he's at they are in abundance.

And so tomorrow is Midsummer's Eve. Yes, I lied, I'm actually writing this letter on Monday, three days past the due date, but hey, sue me! I'm sure Alan would be proud. I'm born on the Walpurgisnacht (also a mini-lie) and apparently the Midsummer's Eve is supposedly equally witchy as the latter. I think this day is also a little bit Alan's day, as he was nothing short of an excellent witch—maybe even a communication witch (or connector witch, which?), a communication mischief expert, a little bit supernatural.

So apparently even a boring scam letter can turn out to be something. I'll make sure to read them more carefully from now onwards, maybe even send a few. I'll also make sure to send out more snail mail, just like I'm writing one to you now.

So where was I...

I'm told this autumn a new MA programme will open at the Estonian Academy of the Arts. It is centred around 'making things public'. I quite like it. I guess I'm also a things-public-maker of sorts (though compared to Alan there's a helluva long way to go), and I'd like to explore this more (maybe with your help?). Sometimes I think it's difficult to balance between making other people's things public and making things public on and of my own. But hey, we're all learning here (by the way, right now, while sitting here in my mother's yard I can hear an ice-cream (*I will have the mocha cheep, with the mocha and the cheep!*[2]—shout out to Andy Kaufman) truck pass by—somehow I think that is an excellent things-public-maker).

This spring, having to reluctantly take on online teaching and the additional occupation of behind-the-curtains (literally) psychologist, I decided we should collectively explore our windows. I was really into all this clapping[3] that was happening all around and thought that's basically all we should be looking into. Deprived of all our physical communication tools, the windows seemed like the last bit of space that could be occupied with personal expression. What a ride that turned out to be—for several weeks we met every Thursday morning on our screens to discuss what each of them had prepared. The outcome was extremely colourful, with piano recitals, window yoga-classes, flags, banners and so and so on springing up like mushrooms; the window space was extended to the elevator, supermarket and pavement (shout out to all my kiddos-and-sort-of friends at the KABK in the Hague).

I miss there being more of this haphazard making things public. Alan took his public-things-making to the streets, books, newspapers, and the TV screen. The messages were mixed, sometimes very straight-forward, and other times more abstract... but what it never was was short of funny.

Dear friend, what a year it's been so far. I'm very proud of you for all your hard work and patience. In September we'll pick up the pieces again, in one form or another, and one location or another. I'll be watching you! And I hope you and me, we'll both make public, funny or not.

Take care, sporing upgathered,

1. An email from Alan Abel, which I'm doubtful would be his real email wherever he is at this very moment, though how can we be sure ghosts don't have email addresses?
2. Zehme, Bill. *Lost in the Funhouse: The Life and Mind of Andy Kaufman*, New York: Delacorte Press, 1999
3. In the early months of the COVID-19 pandemic, several cities and neighbourhoods in Europe organised mass clapping events in support of the front-line healthcare workers.

Dear Friend vol 16, July 2020, written by Alicia Olushola Ajayi, designed by Ott Kagovere, edited by Rachel Kinbar, image "power hungry_2020 self-portrait" by Alicia Ajayi,
concept by Sandra Nuut & Ott Kagovere, title font Cap Sizun by Eva Rank, text font Ladna Sans by Andree Paat (Kirjatehnika), p
ublished by Estonian Academy of Arts, Department of Graphic Design, thanks to Indrek Sirkel and Partel Eelmere. Previous issues at gd.artun.ee/dearfriend

POWER-HUNGRY FREEDOM DEFICIENT BLACKITY BLACK VIRAL RE-ENACTMENT

✱✱ DEAR FRIEND,

You good sis??!! I hope you're up on your stretching game, finding ways to keep sane, finding ways to escape, finding other ways to express whatever you feel while staying hydrated. While talking to a friend today, I was reminded of how I can be restricted by an ideal of freedom. It's the kind of life lesson that I keep having to relearn. And each time it comes crashing down on me like a ton of bricks or another Kanye tweet. In the last few months, Black freedom seems to be conveniently nested into popular headlines or company messaging dominating our feeds. This recent flare of attention given to generations-old call for Black liberation has been all-encompassing and sudden, yet familiar in other ways. But I was reminded by my friend today that freedom is not the same as power.

Wanting freedom is an ancestral tick steeped in Black folk's DNA. It's the constant asking of Black people to speak out and speak up, to make public declarations of wanting freedom that's new—for me at least. As if me trying to do more than nail the perfect twist out method and survive in a world with skin as dark as the sweetest of berries isn't already enough? Recently regulated to my small Brooklyn apartment, much of my idle time was filled with the trauma of trying to remember all of the names of those who lost their freedom because of the color of their skin. I also reflected on how white empathy seems only to be sparked by gruesome images of Black pain as the video of George Floyd's murder went "viral."

Many took to the streets and co-opted the only public spaces available to demonstrate against white supremacy. Even more took to their keyboards to root for Black liberation. There were beautifully crafted ads in support of... who knows?, lengthy "do better" posts about humanity, and abstract black squares. There were also thoughtful think pieces, courageous self-reflections, and incredibly moving art. I didn't *do* any of this. I couldn't even bring myself to do the smallest act of hitting the like button for much of what I saw. I used the "stay at home" order as a veil to disappear, not committing to investing in the energy of the moment. I felt paralyzed by consumption. And as the streets swelled with people across the US, I grew skeptical of the scores of young white faces I saw in these crowds. Then came the messages.

wf*: "How are you doing?"
Me: "It has been overwhelming and rough."

wf = random white friend I met the week before the pandemic shut down*

This response was all the honesty and energy I was willing to muster up. But in my head, that energy was on a whole other level...

***Alicia's brain re-enactment of a conversation that never happened...*

wf: "How are you doing?"
Me: "It has been overwhelming and rough. But it has been overwhelming and rough for a while. I recently learned how slave and free states regulated the movement of enslaved AND freed Blacks during the antebellum period. I was shocked at my ignorance of this history, but I was also shocked at all the ways that policies and laws have evolved to be less detected and only in service to guarantee Black freedom never means Black power. So my question back to you is, "How are you doing with all of this? Have you figured out your part in this yet? What is it about Black power that is so unsettling? What power are you willing to give up so that Black power can have a fighting chance? How are you ok with your part in this?"

But I never go that far because I dread the answer, and part of me already knows it, and the other part could care less. The next few weeks were met with a different yet more thoughtful question as the streets grew louder.

wf: "How can I dismantle white supremacist systems of oppression? What can I do about it?"
Me: *silence*

***another re-enactment*

wf: "How can I dismantle white supremacist systems of oppression? What can I do about it?"
Me: "How the fuck should I know??!! I didn't make this shit. FIGURE IT OUT for your own humanity's sake. Please don't ask me to do any more work on tearing down what you and yours have spent generations fortifying!"

Again I don't have the energy, or perhaps it is the courage that I lack. Either way, my silence sits there in awkward text exchanges and Zoom calls. It's easy to get lost in all the ways I wish to be free as a young, ambitious, self-indulgent, angry, joyous, generous, hurt, loving, spirited, analytical, determined Black woman. But what would it look like if I exchanged the desire for freedom for the lust of power? We have a strange idea of the concept of power. It's almost always tied to control, oppression, capitalism, whiteness, penises, etc. And there have been so many times when I have been conditioned not to demand power. But like many concepts and theories, Blacks have to redefine it for themselves. What does it mean to desire power from a place of love? What would it feel like to let the words leave my lips? What would it look like to carry that energy with me wherever I went? Freedom is the bare minimum, and I want more for my life and my community. I want power.

Dear Friend vol 17, August 2020, written by Maria Juur, image of a selection of Kastner-Kahn houses and the town synagogue (center row, first image on the right) in Roosevelt, NJ, by Maria Juur, designed by Ott Kagovere, edited by Rachel Kinbar, concept by Sandra Nuut & Ott Kagovere, title font Cap Sizun by Eva Rank, text font Ladna Sans by Andree Paat (Kirjatehnika), published by Estonian Academy of Arts, Department of Graphic Design, thanks to Indrek Sirkel and Pärtel Eelmere. Previous issues at gd.artun.ee/dearfriend

NEW JERSEY

BAUHAUS

ESTONIAN-AMERICAN

KIBBUTZ

DEAR FRIEND,

I hope you are staying safe and well. I am writing these lines from my self-imposed corona-exile in central New Jersey, from a town called Roosevelt (population: 800). Nick and I decided to leave Los Angeles and drive 3000 miles (5000 km) cross-country to spend the summer at his family's cabin in Woodstock, New York—yes, *that* Woodstock—but this week we are house-sitting at his parents' place in rural New Jersey. This week, on August 20th, I also celebrated the Estonian Restoration of Independence Day. It's crazy to me how much New Jersey looks like Estonia (there's even an Estonian house 20 minutes away and former Estonian President T.H. Ilves grew up not far from here), and yet I feel farther from home than ever—mostly due to COVID and the fact that August 20th also marks my 10-year anniversary as an *émigré*, an immigrant by choice.

When I first started dating Nick, he tried explaining to me where he was from. It's not that I wasn't interested, but I've been to my fair share of American small towns, and when he mentioned that his place of birth was only one hour from both New York City and Philadelphia, I remember feeling a bit disappointed that he wasn't from NYC proper, because that would have meant I'd always have a place to stay in the Big Apple. Little did I know that I was actually about to discover one of my favorite places in the U.S., a town that also has an interesting connection to Estonia.

So when Sandra, an old friend from college, asked me put on my art critic hat once again, it quickly dawned on me that I should write about Roosevelt, NJ. Roosevelt (a.k.a. Jersey Homesteads) was created as part of President F.D. Roosevelt's New Deal program to break out of the Great Depression of the 1930s. Nearby Princeton, NJ, resident and university professor Albert Einstein—yes, *that* Einstein—gave the town his political and moral support. Established in 1937, Roosevelt was like an American *kibbutz* for Jewish garment workers, the country's first and only secular Jewish commune funded by U.S. government. [A *kibbutz* is a collective community in Israel that was traditionally based on agriculture. The Israeli *kibbutz* has long been regarded as a successful utopian experiment in communal living.]

Once the plan for Roosevelt was approved, the German-born architect Alfred Kastner was hired to design a factory, a community building, and a few hundred houses. He, in turn, reached out to the Estonian-born architect Louis Kahn and hired him as his principal assistant. Somehow, I left Estonia, moved to the States, and ended up marrying a guy who grew up in a house designed by an Estonian architect. *What are the odds?!*

Needless to say, Estonians are obsessed with Louis Kahn and his connection to Saaremaa. I am, too. I mean, the guy's a genius. When I look at pictures of Kahn's National Assembly building in Bangladesh, I want to gasp for air and cry. Our lives are just blips in eternity, but concrete monuments like this are forever. Or they should be, at least. I've visited a handful of Kahn buildings in the U.S. and it always feels special—even when lurking and loitering around the Salk Institute in San Diego on a day when it's closed to the public, with my architecture-fanatic mom who was visiting from Estonia.

Kahn worked on Roosevelt at the very beginning of his career when he was strongly influenced by Bauhaus and Le Corbusier. As a result, Roosevelt's homes look like LEGO-houses: they are cinder block rectangles, originally painted white, with flat roofs. They are attached and detached, mostly one story. All the original houses in the town looked alike.

It's so funny and interesting to me how what we value in architecture changes over time. When Roosevelt was created, it marked a moment of hope and renewal amidst a financial and societal crisis, carried by Modernist and utopian ideas. It marked a return to nature from cities (Roosevelt is surrounded by a wildlife conservation area), and a return to safety for the Jewish community. To this day, Roosevelt only has a borough hall, a school, a post office, and a synagogue; the town has no stores. But Roosevelt is no longer a strictly Jewish hub, and you'll have to put in some work to spot an original, unaltered Kahn building on your drive through the town in 2020.

Nick explained to me how when he was a teen, his life was made hell by his parents' project that entailed adding a second story to their original Kahn house. The construction, chaos, and noise went on and on—and his house was not the only one getting a makeover. Many of the original Kahn houses now sport all types of add-ons and features that are a far cry from what we would term "Bauhaus." For me, an Estonian with an Art History degree and reverence for Kahn, this is pure blasphemy. A *butchering* of Bauhaus. Suburbanites' attack on architecture with a capital "A." But the good people of Roosevelt just needed more storage or another bedroom. Roosevelt houses are notorious for not having basements or attics, and so I cannot really blame families who needed more space for taking matters into their own hands.

I love Roosevelt. I love the homes, the history, and the nature. The crickets here at night are so loud I cannot even hear my own thoughts. I forgot to mention that my husband's mom is the mayor of the town, which technically makes me the Crown Princess of Roosevelt, NJ. I hereby extend an invite to you to come visit this very special place. Wishing you a great end-of-summer until we meet again.

Dear Friend vol 18, September 2020, written by Paul John, image "March 3rd—July 8th 2020" by Paul John, designed by Ott Kagovere, edited by Rachel Kinbar, concept by Sandra Nuut & Ott Kagovere, title font Cap Sizun by Eva Rank, text font Ladna Sans by Andree Paat (Kirjatehnika), published by Estonian Academy of Arts, Department of Graphic Design, thanks to Indrek Sirkel and Pärtel Eelmere. Previous issues at gd.artun.ee/dearfriend

DEAR FRIEND,

Walking in New York with my camera is better than having a diary.

My pictures are like dreams, overlaid and blurry at times. The film has been exposed multiple times, and there's no record of its history. I look at a picture and try to remember where I was and when I clicked. When did I finish that roll? I'm noticing little details that give way to some memory.

Did it fly back with me before I snapped the last few shots to send off to get developed? Or maybe I took a long detour from the subway to walk?

I haven't had a metro day in a very long time. Perhaps that's what I miss most about the before times: a day filled with subways and walking. I'd walk from my studio to my favorite independent book store, Printed Matter, for a reading, quickly run into Chelsea to see some openings, hustle once more to the Lower East Side and catch the end of a friends' performance, then leisurely trot over to a bar, let's say Clandestino (the grumpy bartender liked me... I think), or maybe walk up to the East Village and have a drink at Blue & Gold Tavern, where everything is five dollars or less. It's surprisingly tidy for a dive bar, and they have chess boards built into their tables. I'd always ask the bartender for the chess pieces, trading my ID as collateral, and await a stranger to play. I'd lose a lot, sometimes on purpose, but mostly because I am not improving in chess. Winning isn't as much fun as playing.

Most nights, I'd walk alone hoping to run into a friendly face: old restaurant friend, old colleague, old secondary school alum, and filling with excitement when meeting someone new, eager to know who they are and what stories they have. I'm reminiscing about nights I'd walk into KTown dreaming of doing karaoke by myself, but instead I'd walk back to my studio in Hell's Kitchen and play music as loud as I could.

Every time I think I have some time, it gets eaten. I was busy before. It was in vogue to be busy, and today I thought, "Wow, what a time. I can't be busy..."

I'm still trying to say something, but I can't do it briefly.

I found a way to get busy while New York was in shutdown. We decided to run the annual Brooklyn Art Book Fair online to support independent publishers in our community, most of which are under-represented and marginalized, but some have loads of visibility. All these various publishers and artists had taken on financial investments and prepared new work only to be presented with a vacuum to exhibit them, as the Los Angeles Art Book Fair had just been cancelled and the shutdowns began around the world. We began with "what if we can't host the fair in May, IRL..." and developed a new plan from scratch. Our weekly video calls *almost* felt like we were in the studio. I want to keep the memories of calling all of them and talking to them about this fair, but they are disintegrating. When the protests erupted, we were on the phone for almost an entire day straight. It was an emotional day and laborious week. But ultimately we put our energies there, to the street, in print, and postponed the fair. I'm still feeling the weight, under my eyes, from that week.

Our fair's mission has always been to lessen the burden on our vendors. We took on the task of completing all the shipping and fulfillment for this online book fair. It was basically a large online store with 45+ vendors and over 400 unique items. We had no idea what to expect, and when sales became overwhelming, we joked about closing the fair early (we didn't). All the vendors shipped their sold inventory to us and we picked, packed, and shipped the orders to their final destination. We made our own fulfillment world in the printshop. Etching presses filled up with inventory, ink slabs became packing stations, and I made a karaoke station with our portable PA while we sent out almost 800 packages of books, prints, and merchandise.

How many hours did we work on that project? Can you honestly say that you stopped working if you worked in your dreams?

I'm trying to remember that you can touch fire, and not get burned... you just can't hold onto it.

I'm meant to say more, but I can't. It's impossible. Maybe we can meet one day at the Robert Blackburn Printmaking Workshop for a glance at the most important histories in art and printmaking. We can walk to Printed Matter, cut over to the Center for Book Arts, then hop down to Scarr's for a slice, to Attaboy to see Jon or The Smith to see Doug, while I tell you how Bob would change lives through printmaking, and later we can talk about whatever we want, jaywalking across streets and dipping between cars and then down into the subway, chasing *something* worth working towards.

I remember asking people visiting the city, "Do you have an unlimited weekly? Get one..." Secretly hoping they come on this journey with me through Manhattan by foot and trolly.

I prefer telling stories; I'm better with showing pictures. They offer me a more poetic way to understand the constant madness surrounding me... and this spiral into madness doesn't seem to end. I know life only goes one way. All my friends are leaving me... they're leaving New York. Nobody lives here to spend time in their 9 square meter room, they're here for the streets, the people, the never ending list of things to do and eat... some things are meant to dissolve, others to vanish with the wind, "*New York, I love you, but you're bringing me down...*"

If you feel like it, call me and I can tell you all the stories I know and all the stories I wish I knew more about.

** this was written from June → September 2020... **

TRYING BRIEFLY REMEMBER DISINTEGRATING EATEN DREAMS IMPOSSIBLE

Dear Friend vol 19, October 2020, written by Tuomas Kortteinen, image "Folkestone Gardens, 2020" by Tuomas Kortteinen, designed by Ott Kagovere, edited by Rachel Kinbar, concept by Sandra Nuut & Ott Kagovere, title font Cap Sizun by Eva Rank, text font Ladna Sans by Andree Paat (Kirjatehnika), published by Estonian Academy of Arts, Department of Graphic Design, thanks to Indrek Sirkel and Pärtel Eelmere. Previous issues at gd.artun.ee/dearfriend

✱✱

DEAR FRIEND,

GUILT

I imagine you can relate: we recently moved from a large European city where almost everyone spoke English to a small European city where everyone speaks the language we grew up with. Partly because of Covid, partly because it was time, partly because of money.

The first thing to return was a pervasive sense of anticipatory guilt. Before moving, our first language had been only spoken at home with my partner, on the phone with my parents, or down in the pub with Esa. This had been a language of nurturing, affirmation and collective ranting: a language of care. Now, the same language was everywhere, but it was a language of blame and enforcement, which quickly colonised our insides. The guilt wasn't for anything we had done, it was for everything else: being was *being towards* being judged. But these rules had been created together, and this was the language we'd grown up with—how could we complain?

RANTING

✱ ✱ ✱

FREEDOM

I began thinking that this collective guilt was like an invisible, ever-growing lattice of moss that covered everything, everywhere, and maybe I had just not been perceiving it in the large European city in the same way I was perceiving it here. Maybe that moss was an excretion of language, and I simply wasn't immersed enough in English to be affected.

In any case, the point is this: in English, I had felt freer. It hadn't bothered me that whenever the native speakers said 'we', I was never sure if I was included or excluded. The International Art School English had bothered me at first, but after a while it turned into a spectacular game of alchemy and ellipsis, where meaning was occasionally brushed against—but never organised into—enforced units. Communication was difficult but with wider horizons than I had been accustomed to. In hindsight I wish I didn't take it all so seriously back then.

ENGLISH

I think partly the reason I'd felt so free was because lots of the connotative baggage—the dead weight of an over-extended sense of self-reflection—was suddenly gone, or at least completely non-applicable. I could write, I could speak, I could text, all without worrying about who or what my choice of register reminded the recipient of. The tradition of all dead generations no longer weighed like a nightmare on the brain of the living.

LIDL

What makes English wonderful for second-language speakers is that it takes from everywhere, you can add from anywhere, and no one speaks it perfectly. And if they do, they're the minority, and so soft-spoken and polite that it doesn't really matter (or: they would never dream of explicitly enforcing their orthographic views on the rest of us). English homogenises, but it's also a place where you can escape, both from yourself and your first language:

OPAQUE

"I value too much our beautiful Polish literature to introduce into it my worthless twaddle. But for Englishmen my capacities are just sufficient: they enable me to earn my living." (Joseph Conrad)

What is key here is the notion of sufficiency. English seems to be an evidently sufficient language. English is often like going to Lidl or Aldi: you know you'll get everything you 'need', even though it might not be exactly what you 'desire'. There might be special weeks now and then, but otherwise—for anything unusual—you have to venture out a bit further. But it's so cheap! Feel free to stack your basket all the way to the brim!

But when can you say someone's use of language is sufficient, and to what purpose? The relative ubiquity of English and the multitude of its uses and users has (at least from my privileged position) removed the possibility for external authorities to have any meaningful say on this. Instead, discussions on what is sufficient or what is elegant are best left to the participants of the individual communicative act itself, which can then become a joyful discussion on language itself:

"It's as though one friend says to another, "How good it is to say 'How are you?'" The other replying, 'When I answer "I am well and how are you," what I really mean is that I'm delighted to have a chance to say these familiar things—they bridge the lonely distances.'" (Don DeLillo, *The Names*)

However, it's not just about the familiar things. Like most languages, English is at its best around the edges, when things are just about to snap off the grid. When we run out of words, when we start using words we don't quite know how to pronounce (or all the meanings of)—when the sufficiency of English words is no longer sufficient in terms of what we want to say.

This is what I miss the most, and what I've found the most difficult to replicate.

✱ ✱ ✱

They gathered around the table, tore pizza to pieces, added sriracha mayo, wiped mouths with backs of hands, shared toilet roll, leaned elbows on tables, chewed with mouths open, pointed oily digits at each other. They spoke in accented English about how crazy it all was nowadays. When they were trying to articulate something delicate that they deeply cared about, they found that English would not do. Even though English was a necessary condition of their friendship it wasn't a sufficient one. So they dropped in a word of Romanian, Swedish, Finnish, Portuguese, Greek, Korean. The word was translated and repeated, it was whirled around mouths, examined and compared. It felt like a gift, like an opaque piece of glass that fit the palm of your hand perfectly. It felt like a True Name, a name that connected language and the world and expanded them both in a way English was incapable of doing. Then they continued in English.

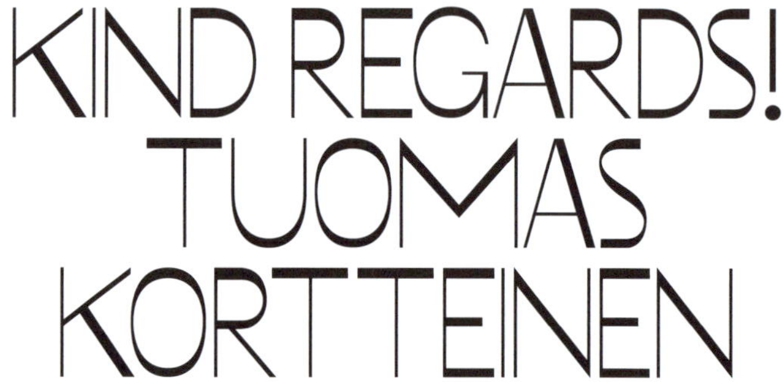

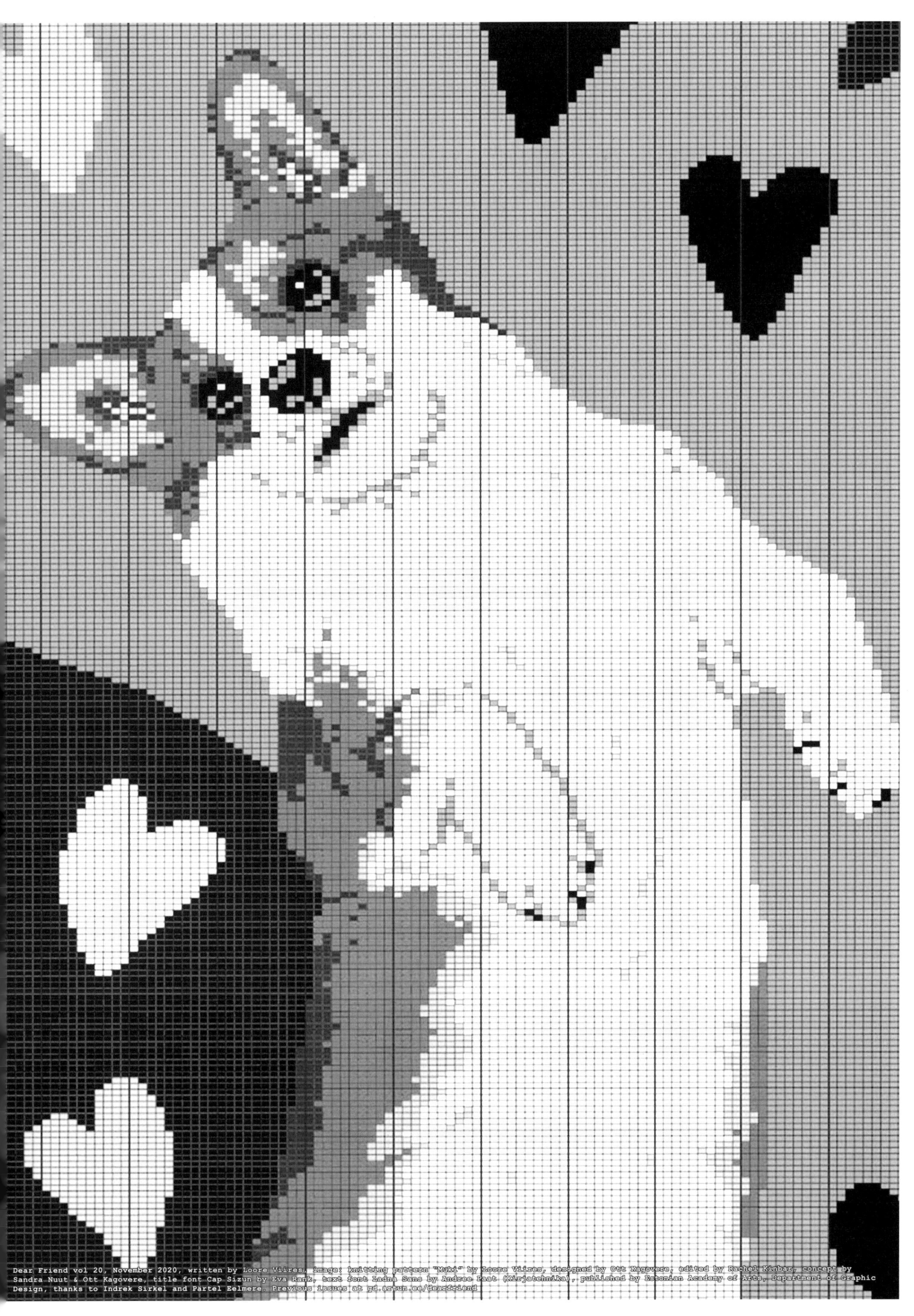

Dear Friend vol 20, November 2020, written by Loore Viires, image: knitting pattern "Muki" by Loore Viires, designed by Ott Kagovere, edited by Rachel Kinbar, concept by Sandra Nuut & Ott Kagovere, title font Cap Sizun by Eva Rank, text font Ladna Sans by Andree Paat (Kirjatehnika), published by Estonian Academy of Arts, Department of Graphic Design, thanks to Indrek Sirkel and Pärtel Eelmere. Previous issues at gd.artun.ee/dearfriend

RUPERT HOLMES FAILURES SELF-CARE JOURNALING PROCRASTINATION KNITTING THERAPY FORGIVENESS

DEAR FRIEND,

Do you like Rupert Holmes? I do, and unironically. I know his songs are often quite silly, occasionally incredibly mundane (*Lunch Hour*, anybody?!), and sometimes so ultra-cinematic that it's tricky to find the right situation in which to listen to them (a prime example of this is his song about a tropical cocktail, which I'm sure you've heard before). I especially like his song *The Place Where Failure Goes* because of its choice of topic—it poignantly talks about the afterlife of creative disappointments.

I've never really wanted to give my own non-success much thought, but I do perpetually feel the weight of my half-finished projects that have accumulated over the years. Right now I recall an unfinished knitted sock somewhere on my shelf, some randomly shaped pieces of plywood in a bag under the bed (a symptom of a not-fully-crafted plan to start making abstract *Hampelmanns*), and a half-painted clay figurine intended for a friend's birthday that was in May. I may know where they're stored physically, but I have trouble pinning them down mentally and fear what they might say about me, if given a voice. Perhaps they linger on in some dark place, akin to Gollum, resenting me for their unfulfilled state?

My latest creative failure has to do with writing. I've never really had a connection with the practice of laying out my intimate thoughts and feelings on paper, aside from a few failed attempts at keeping a journal. Looking back, I've realised that in those instances I wrote with the possibility of someone reading my diary, which resulted in a toned-down version of events and feelings. I usually got bored of keeping a diary on the second day or so, since listing my daily activities was not the most intriguing pursuit. Thus I've ended up with a collection of notebooks, filled only until the third page and then left untouched. They are a constant reminder of my inability to finish things, and for some reason, I can't bring myself to tear out the used pages and repurpose the notebooks. Perhaps I keep them for the purposes of intimidation, sort of like a head on a spike? In any case, this *memento mori* of all my unfinished creative projects is a fitting reminder of my habit of procrastination.

A while back I encountered Julia Cameron's book *The Artist's Way*. Have you heard of it, or maybe even worked through it? In short, it is a self help book intended for everyone within the creative field, originally published in the 1990s. When I first skimmed it, I figured that it needs a type of focus and follow-through for which I need to prepare in advance. The book is comprised of reading chapters, a daily writing exercise, a weekly creative assignment and a list of smaller tasks, all of which requires at least an hour-long commitment every day for three months. It seemed like serious business, and I wanted to approach it without setting myself up for failure. My first instinct, brought forth also by the aforementioned unfinished notebooks, was to invite friends to take part with me. I always feel more responsible when others are involved and there is someone to report to, so I talked my husband Oskar into joining me.

As you've probably already realised, we sort of failed in this undertaking. My approach to getting things done reminds me of the story from Apuleius's *Metamorphoses*, where Venus sets up four near-impossible assignments for her future daughter-in-law, Psyche. Psyche sets out to fulfil these duties, but breaks down every time, halfway into solving them. When she's asked to sort a pile of seeds or gather wool from the Golden Fleece, she lays down, starts to cry and wishes to die. Yet every time mythical forces, such as tiny ants or a talking reed plant, help her out and suggest the smartest choice of action. Us mortals don't always have mythical beings around to help us with the task at hand like she did, but I do find it amusing that there exists such a deeply relatable mythical character, sort of like a procrastinator-goddess.

Much like her, some days it just didn't feel right to continue with the book or to start writing, so I put off the assignments until the next week. The biggest struggle throughout was the daily monster-excercise—the backbone of the program—known as *morning pages*, where three pages' worth of text is to be handwritten every morning, before doing anything else. We bought new, proper-looking notebooks and decided to keep with it, no matter what. But as you know, one does not change their whole way of operating in the course of one day, and neither did we. What actually started was a long, exhausting process of trial and error, with stretches of self-loathing and eventual self-acceptance. This on-again, off-again approach to the program probably didn't do it justice, but I'm glad to turn back to writing every once in a while. I grew to really love the freedom of filling pages with text and never looking at them again. It worked wonders on the inner critic who is normally pointing fingers at everything I do, the main culprit of this postponing life-style. I also started noticing some very welcome changes—I got increasingly fed up with complaining about the same things over and over, which, in turn, urged me to solve my issues even if just to avoid ever writing about them again.

So, after writing about knitting my sister-in-law a scarf for Christmas for the millionth time, I began with my current project—a corgi-patterned scarf that takes about a month's worth of mornings to make. It's quite a cheerful project and has helped me regain confidence in my ability to complete things. Perhaps when it's done I'll return to the morning writing practice again, until another project comes to mind that I feel determined enough to undertake.

To come back to the song once more, I am kind of heart-warmed by the line: "This is where all the might-have-beens triumph and forgive". I hope my own projects are this understanding.

BEST WISHES!
LOORE VIRES

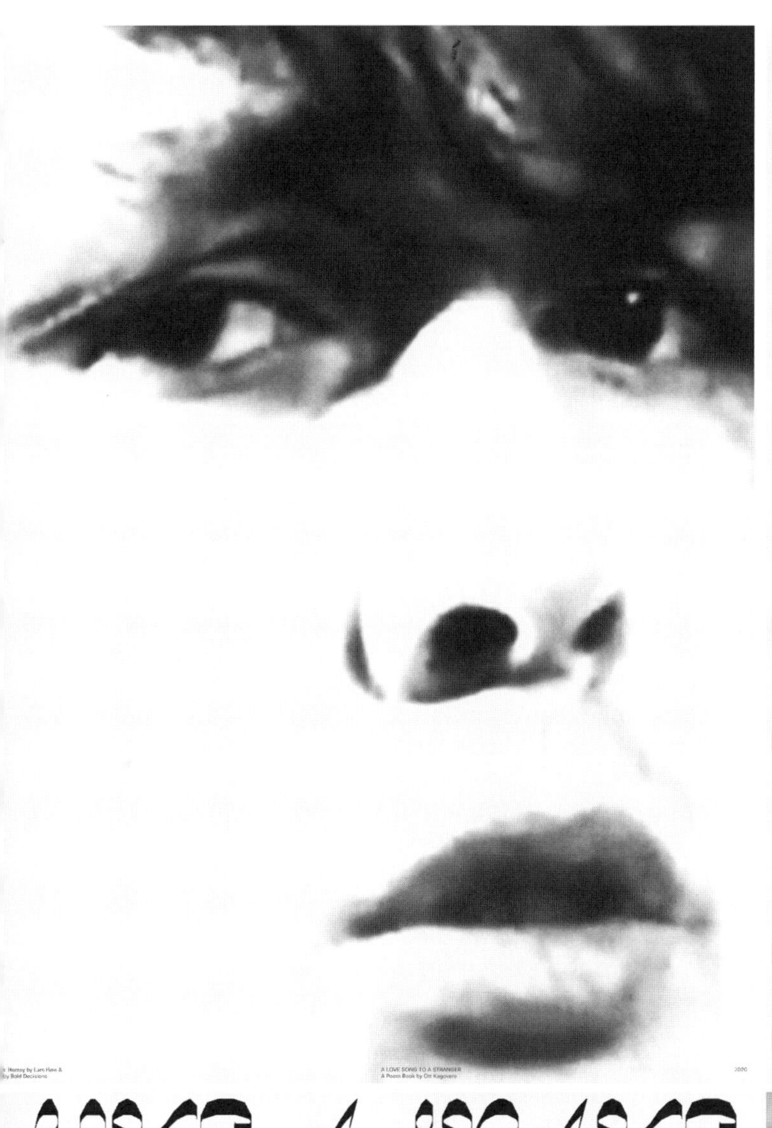

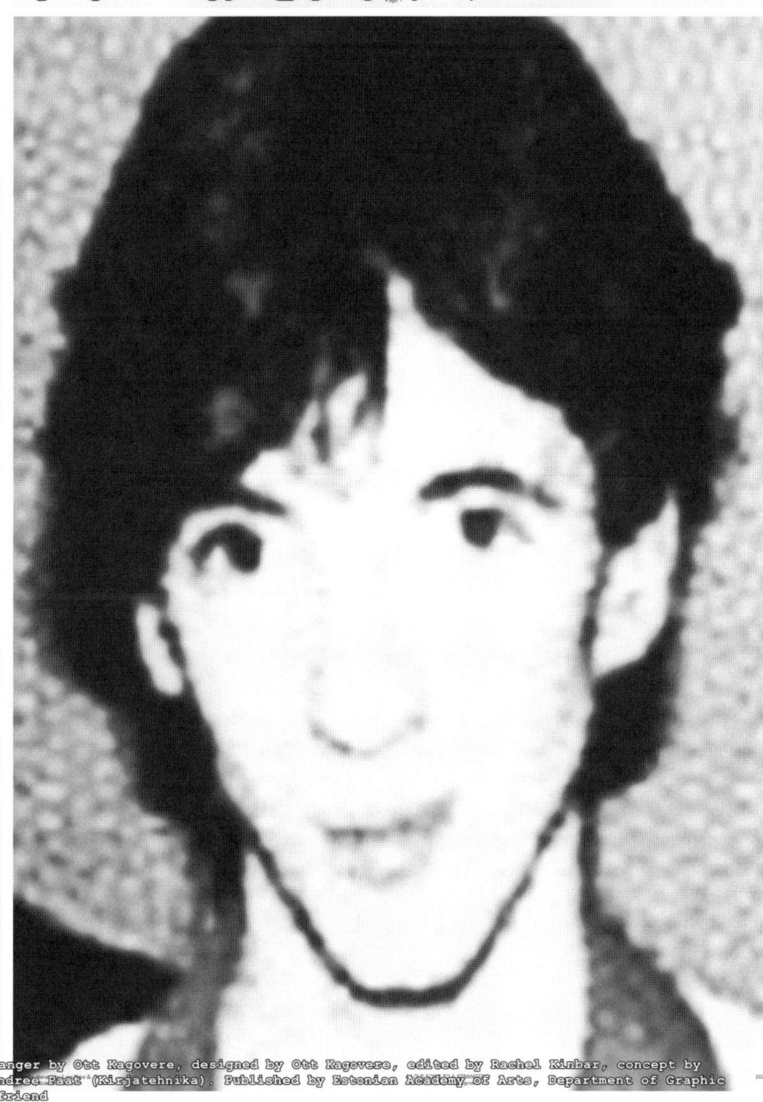

Dear Friend vol 21, December 2020. Written by Ott Kagovere, image: A Love Song to a Stranger by Ott Kagovere, designed by Ott Kagovere, edited by Rachel Kinbar, concept by Sandra Nuut & Ott Kagovere, title font Cap Sizun by Eva Rank, text font Ladna Sans by Andree Paat (Kirjatehnika). Published by Estonian Academy of Arts, Department of Graphic Design. Thanks to Indrek Sirkel and Pärtel Eelmere. Previous issues at gd.artun.ee/dearfriend

PUNCTUATION MARKS

ERIK SATIE

TIME AS METHOD

FEMINISM FOR MEN

KALI MALONE

DEAR FRIEND,

I want to talk to you about poetry. How words are like small images and sentences like collections of them—small books or pamphlets. In poetry, though, I am not sure if we actually have sentences, because most of it has abandoned initial capitals and punctuation. Perhaps that kind of poetry is pure language, not language that is divided into equally digestible parts by capitals and commas.

I recently self-published a poem of mine, and it has made me reflect on several things. It took me around two years to materialise this small publication and the process made me think of *time as method*. And about how, quite often, I have felt anxious about making something, wishing for instant gratitude and praise. How sometimes there has not been a proper creative impulse behind my work, just the need for feedback and recognition. That made me think of Erik Satie's *Vexations*—a short melody, only a few lines, which is meant to be played 840 times in a row. The performance of this piece lasts for around 18 hours, transforming the brief melody into Wagnerian dimensions. I see a certain similarity here with my poem booklet—a couple of pages of poetry, stretched out over a span of time, providing me with weeks full of experiments and meditations.

Time, in that sense, has a crucial role in graphic design. A role that is sometimes overlooked, due to the fact that traditionally graphic design has not been considered a temporal art. But this notion only makes sense when you exclude the *process* of making, of designing, from the final product. If you avoid this exclusion, as one should, in my opinion, multiple possibilities for temporal experimentation in graphic design open up. If one uses time consciously, one can think of it as a method. Be it something conceptual, like Satie's *Vexations* or something mundane like waiting and taking the time needed. If we still feel uncomfortable talking about graphic design as a temporal art, then so be it. But we should never dismiss it as a processual art.

I also like that the initial impulse behind the work has been utterly designerly. Lars Høie, a friend and colleague of mine, gave me some of his fonts and I was eager to try them out. As I was unable to push them into any of my professional work and was tired of making random zines consisting of found materials (which I had done previously), I lurched into a folder where I keep small writings, notes, and poems of mine and tried to typeset some of them with Heresy—the font I liked the most from Lars.

Hi there, you are beautiful and passionate and your mind is a blast! I am in fever and afraid but leaping of faith, like a snake in the soil, I weep in a moment so fragile so fresh, light as a tender corpse, I undress in the peak of you.

That's the poem. Initially it was slightly different. I rewrote it many times in InDesign to get the right flow to suit the font, the typesetting, and the format of the poster. Again, a very designerly way to write—for and within a specific form(at), as opposed to the "abstract" way poets usually do, as if writing into thin air, without thinking about the actual form that the words will materialise into later.

The poem is entitled *A Love Song to a Stranger*, and my initial idea was to hang them up in the city and the message of the poem would be directed to random passers-by. It expresses my vulnerability that accompanies an expression of love, of care and devotion. I can not think of a more vulnerable utterance. It is as if standing naked, completely open, in front of someone. It reminded me of a small fact I heard about dogs, that when they are defeated in a scuffle they reveal their most vulnerable body part—their throat—to their opponent. As if announcing, *I'm yours now, do as you please*. I have the feeling that love entails a similar scuffle. But not necessarily between lovers, but within ourselves. It is a struggle, a quarrel within ourselves to come to terms with accepting love. And when we finally do, we let ourselves be defeated by it, we reveal our most vulnerable selves, for bites and kisses.

The image layer on top of the text is a reflection of the poet, the lover, the naked one. It is a depiction of male vulnerability, which is also something that I have been thinking about for years. Here I have had many ideas for publications and events, one of them being a zine entitled *Feminism for Men*, which collects images of men crying and, as an extension to that, an event where there would be a room full of men, men full of tears. I somehow find this image of men crying very beautiful and empowering. It depicts men as human beings, with all the hurt and vulnerability that comes with that, not men as statues of confidence and conquering. To loosely paraphrase Leslie Gore, *It's my gender and I'll cry if I want to*! But somehow I never managed to materialise these ideas. I always felt that it needed more *time*, more digestion, was too important to be executed in haste.

The images come from another poetry folder that I have, this one consisting only of images, entitled *Mundane Crushes*. It is a collection of screenshots of portraits which have moved me deeply and function as a vessel for small desires, sometimes sexual, but more often emotional and empathic. The first image in the folder was this one of the experimental musician Kali Malone. My reading of it is very poetic—her hair in the wind, eyes slightly wet, the both of us, on the verge of a profound realisation, words unnecessary. I also enjoy the fact that, when written down, those daydreams look silly and adolescent, but as such become refreshing. They allow me to laugh at myself, or rather with myself and deflate the burdensome seriousness that comes with the image of adultness. As if being an adult means being devoid of desire!

I think of the images as an extra set of punctuation marks within the poem, providing small pauses and emphases. It is an extra layer of information which simplifies and clarifies the meaning of the whole. I could go on and on about the poem, but I want to keep this letter shorter than *Vexations*, so perhaps it is better if you read the poem yourself. Let me know if you would like to have it and I'll be glad to send it to you.

DEAR FRIEND 22-32
2021

SANDRA NUUT
✶✶
SHEERE NG
✶✶
MAARIN EKTERMANN
✶✶
ARJA KARHUMAA
✶✶
ROSEN EVELEIGH
✶✶
KAI LOBJAKAS
✶✶

STUART BERTOLOTTI-BAILEY
✶✶
ALICE TWEMLOW
✶✶
MICHELLE MILLAR FISHER*
✶✶
SAARA HANNUS
✶✶
OTT KAGOVERE
✶✶

* Only in letter format

All the previous cover images were selected or designed by the authors of the letters.
From 2021 onwards all the cover visuals were created by invited graphic designers and artists.

Dear Friend vol 22, February 2021. Written by Sandra Nuut, image "Feedback Loop" by Mai Bauvald, designed by Ott Kagovere, edited by Rachel Kinbar, concept by Sandra Nuut & Ott Kagovere, title font Cap Sizun by Eva Rank, text font Ladna Sans by Andree Paat (Kirjatehnika). Published by Estonian Academy of Arts, Department of Graphic Design. Thanks to Indrek Sirkel and Pärtel Eelmere. Previous issues at gd.artun.ee/dearfriend

TRANSFORMATION SAND VALUES ACTING THINGS WAITING

DEAR FRIEND, I suppose I have fallen into some brilliant trap which I continue exploring.

I first thought that it was my fascination with the social polarisation, our inability to meet, and furthermore some desire to solve the impossibilities. Yet, the truth is that I am not looking to meet anyone thinking otherwise, at least today. I have also been intrigued by being misunderstood, my voice getting disturbed or not heard at all. And it is possible that, at times, my hearing might have not been clear enough. You know when you say something and the other reads it in a surprising way? We all experience it. The message does not arrive or click inside the other. Giant steps away from all this fuss is the idea of transformation within, which happens rather rarely because of the circumstances that need to be in place. These are some mixed thoughts that I have been thinking about for a year, maybe more, proof of how painfully slow of a thinker I am. I found a piece that intrigues me in a similar manner —it is complex to comprehend and communicate— it is not impossible, just takes time and a commitment to the idea of reaching change in understanding. It is "Acting Things VII—School of Fluid Measures" by designer Judith Seng.

I first came across this piece in 2018 at the 4th Istanbul Design Biennial, titled "A School of Schools—Design As Learning", and curated by Jan Boelen with Nadine Botha and Vera Sacchetti. "Acting Things VII—School of Fluid Measures", an installation of 18 colourful pyramid-like sand piles in a simultaneously lively and sterile-looking white space, was one of the many "schools" of the biennale. The colourful sand piles have since been presented and explored in different cultural institutions, like Atelier Luma in Arles, France, and Z33, Hasselt, Belgium, and this year hopefully at the Tallinn Art Hall Gallery. This piece is not the first work in the series of "Acting Things", in which Seng explores production processes. She is interested in daily situations and "tries to make these understandable as a work of design—a work that has been shaped, has a form and way of being performed..." Imagine an interaction at home, something as simple as washing the dishes. How is this communicated between the partners and then performed?

"Acting Things VII—School of Fluid Measures" aids us in discussing values through direct interaction with sand. The sand piles carry predetermined meanings or values, such as individuality, collectivity, freedom, responsibility, and standardization (among others) that can be mixed. It is interesting to read the reflections that people have had after a session of physical communication, where roles change in the process of negotiating perspectives. Not much is constant here, and (if you do not pre-coordinate) the results in the sand are unexpected. While working with Judith via Zoom calls on the exhibition for Tallinn, we discuss the different aspects of the work, and over time these calls have turned out to be like shifting sand as each time I get more nuance about the work and her practice.

Picture this. Blue sand on the floor in a perfect triangular pile. You are allowed to touch the pile, push it aside. You feel the grains slipping through your fingers. There is another pile in front of you that is, let's say, yellow, and there is someone that moves these yellow grains toward what was previously your perfect blue pile. The two of you move together in silence, pushing, pulling, stroking, pouring, throwing, sweeping... Ideas reveal and conceal themselves in front of you slowly, clearly, and unclearly, through the process of looking, moving, interacting, and imagining.

We learn to communicate again. It always seems to take time when we touch the boundaries with our kitten paws. We try not to irritate. Then again, sometimes we use claws and make some marks that heal, though some traces remain. This piece in sand gives us the opportunity to refocus and perhaps even disturb our regular ways of communicating and negotiating our daily ways of being. Furthermore, here we focus on the act itself: communicating.

I had another moment of reflection after reading an interview with Wolfgang Tillmans in "Para-Platforms: On the Spatial Politics of Right-Wing Populism", where in the end the artist concludes "complexity and the reality of being different will win." My mind turned a somersault after realising that such an idea is possible, and "Acting Things" reappeared in my mind again. I guess this phrase captures my hope for the forthcoming installation—discussing social constructs and daily situations with an open mind and gentle heart.

But why did I mention transformation in the first place? I and, perhaps you agree, we often tend to have an impulse to try to understand something totally, permanently, in absolute terms. To keep an idea, we restrict ourselves, which can keep us afloat. The trap is this internal fight between dynamic and static. And when change (in values) happens, it can hurt or enrich. I see shifts and sometimes even earthquakes when I am teaching at the Art Academy, possibly one of the best environments for explosions, internal disturbances. Ideas can disrupt the ways students have seen themselves and their lives so far. It happened to me too, and I hope it continues happening. It could be as simple as a text, an artwork, a design discussed in a seminar that turns everything upside down. Sometimes new understanding creeps up on us calmly, when we have the willingness, environment, timing—the right context. But often, in reality understanding may take time.

Have I written a promotional confession? Maybe. Mostly I wish to meet you and learn more about ourselves.

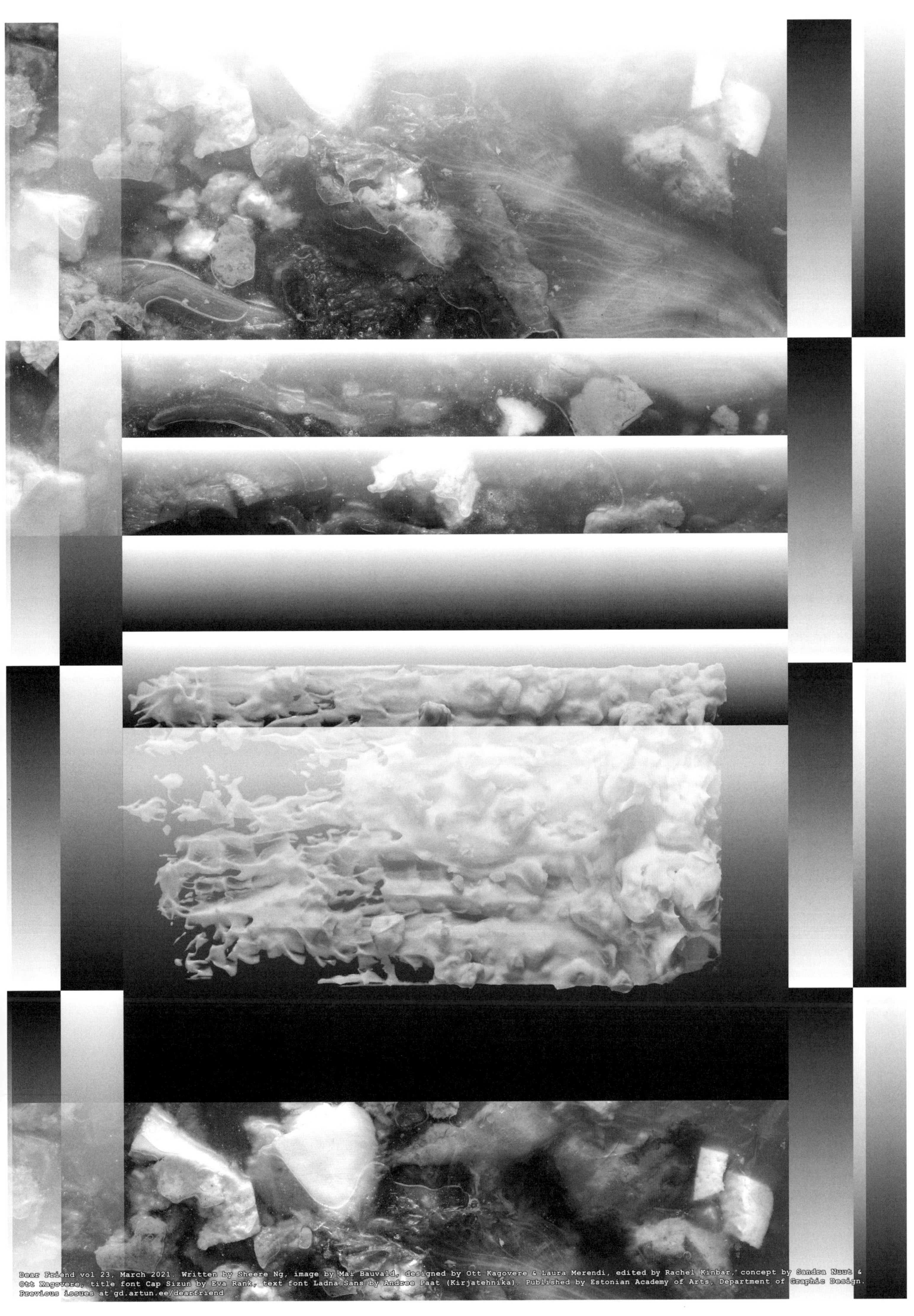

Dear Friend vol 23, March 2021. Written by Sheere Ng, image by Mai Bauvald, designed by Ott Kagovere & Laura Merendi, edited by Rachel Kinbar, concept by Sandra Nuut & Ott Kagovere, title font Cap Sizun by Eva Rank, text font Ladna Sans by Andree Paat (Kirjatehnika). Published by Estonian Academy of Arts, Department of Graphic Design. Previous issues at gd.artun.ee/dearfriend

MASAK

DEAR FRIEND,

The book that I told you about? I finally finished it, nine years after I embarked on this project. I titled it *When Cooking Was A Crime: Masak in the Singapore Prisons, 1970s–80s*.

Masak means "to cook" in Malay. But to former inmates incarcerated during that period, it meant turning chamber pots into cooking pots and blankets into fuel to secretly produce hot, savoury suppers in their cells. I came to know about *masak* by chance. Then an aspiring food writer, I cold-called a restaurateur who was formerly an inmate. I asked to interview him about his experience of prison meals, but he offered to tell me about *masak* instead!

PUNISHMENT

You see, prison food was routinely cold and so repetitive that it became a torture to eat. So, the inmates heated up canned food from the commissaries and mixed them with ingredients they set aside from lunch or dinner. Some even set up traps to catch and cook wild pigeons, rabbits or cats. They devised many ways to set up fire, often resorting to stealing tools or smuggling them from outside the prisons.

A few recipes required no cooking, but were creative nonetheless. Round peanut candies were shaped with a hollow chess piece, and birthday cakes with layers of magazine covers held together by rice glue.

FREEDOM

I gathered so much information, from the first interviewee and the subsequent seven, that it became daunting to organise. To be honest, the combined topic of prison and food requires little editorial effort to stir interest. But I was not keen on sensationalising the story. The study of food and the behaviours around it have created a better understanding of different people and situations. I asked myself: what might *masak* tell us about inmates and prison conditions?

If I wanted to properly analyse my data, I thought, I better use a coding method that I learned in grad school. I shall not bore with you the details, but it eventually helped me identify both the explicit and implicit meanings of food, the latter of which, I believe, the inmates weren't aware themselves. These meanings formed the four chapters of my book: food as punishment, freedom, control and play.

CONTROL

Prison meals were unintentionally punishing to eat because they had to be prepared many hours before meal times. But inmates also had a hand in making the meals dull, because many of them colluded with the inmate cooks to steal ingredients, leaving meagre portions and undesirable meat cuts for the rest.

Masak then became a way for them to produce hot food and recreate the familiar tastes of hawker fare that they no longer had access to. The final product might seem remote from the original, but with a little bit of imagination, it transported them beyond the prison walls.

Making food also gave inmates a sense of control. Imagine having no say over your haircut and even bowel routine. I know I would feel less like a person and more like property. Making food choices—choosing to pair tofu with luncheon meat (spam) instead of canned pig trotter—was a rare act of free will in prisons. It helped restore some dignity to the inmates.

PLAY

Finally, cooking was akin to playing. Even though it was largely seen as women's work in that time, inmates never saw *masak* as feminine. Instead, they thought it was fun because it required them to break several rules and play a game of cat-and-mouse with the guards. Some food even became an object of play in itself. Rumour has it that some inmates used raw squids for masturbation to simulate a wet vagina! While the account was disputed, many inmates refused to eat squid rings that were of the "right" size.

As you can see, I collected many interesting anecdotes. But however well I can write, the book would be incomplete without pictures to illustrate the inmates' creations. There were no visual records of the items, so nobody, except the inmates, knew what they looked like.

Luckily, I found Don. He is not only a competent photographer, but was also very keen on reproducing the recipes and tools from scratch. He said going through the process would allow him to experience the inmates' frustrations and successes. So, he scraped a can against the floor to open it with his bare hands, and sharpened a chicken bone against the wall to make a shiv. By the end of the photoshoot, which took him the entire lockdown period last year, there were many holes and scratch marks in his home. But Don was pleased. This tedious exercise gave us a glimpse of the extent of the inmates' depravity and boredom.

The thing that I least expected to be challenging was food styling. Conventional food photography entices, but that was not our goal for the book. In Don's words, "it should appease curiosity, rather than evoke appetite". We were therefore careful to avoid the food magazine look, but that was tough. A single dish against a black background tends to look gourmet. But I think we eventually managed that by focusing on making the ingredients recognisable, so that people can appreciate the inmates' ingenuity in improvising with available resources.

Also, instead of using plates and bowls that could make a *masak* dish unnecessarily fancy, we packed them into transparent plastic bags and shot the food through the bags.

The book was finally published in December last year, but my work, my friend, is not over. I now have to go around asking bookstores if they want to carry it. I have also been pitching it to the media. Urgh, it's such a bummer to discuss money right after the euphoria of creating original content. I wish I could just sit back and wait for people to discover it. But that's not good for business, is it? So, here's where you can show your support: *shop.inplainwords.sg*

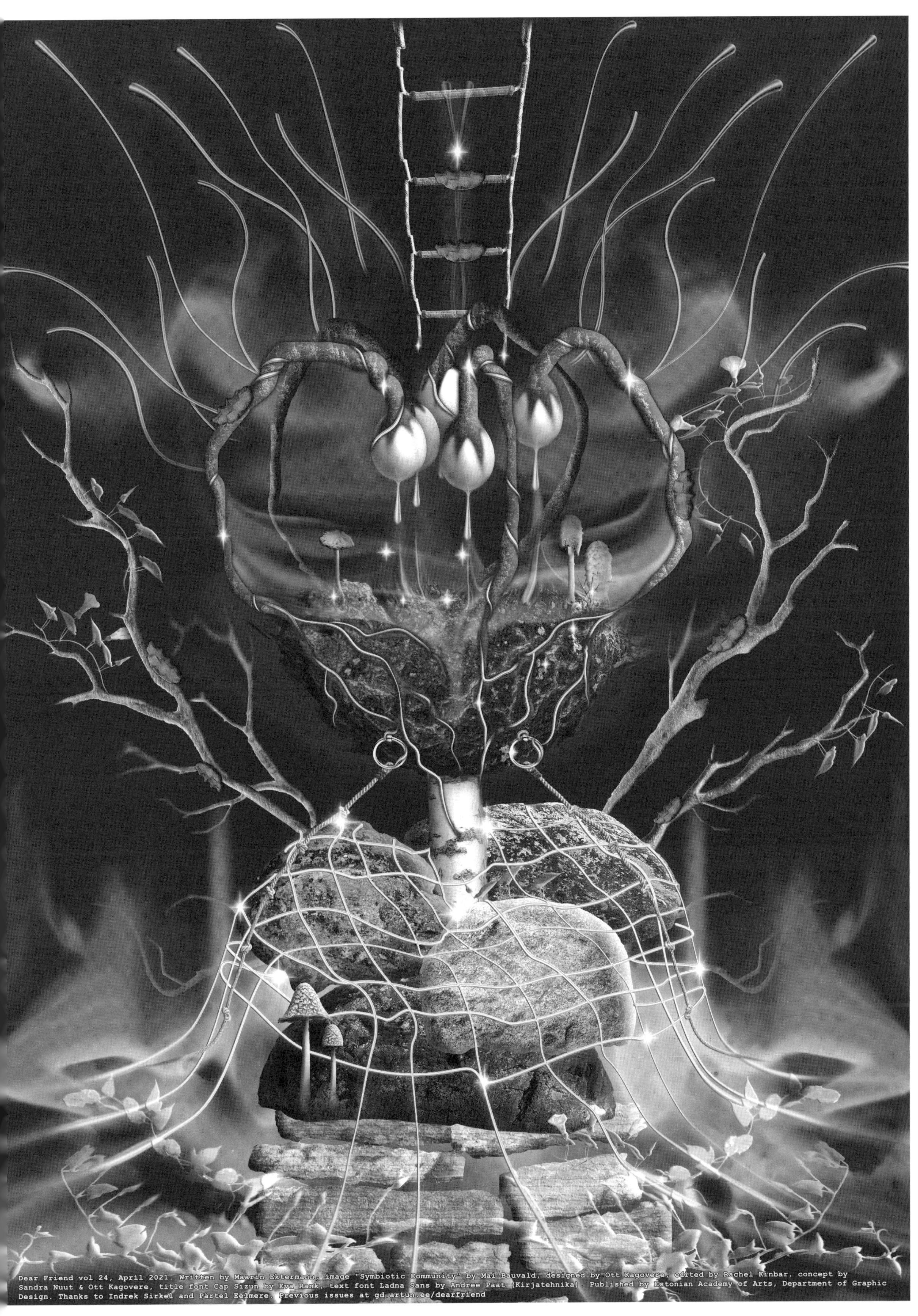

Dear Friend vol 24, April 2021. Written by Maarin Ektermann, image "Symbiotic Community" by Mai Bauvald, designed by Ott Kagovere, edited by Rachel Kinbar, concept by Sandra Nuut & Ott Kagovere, title font Cap Sizun by Eva Rank, text font Ladna Sans by Andree Paat (Kirjatehnika). Published by Estonian Academy of Arts, Department of Graphic Design. Thanks to Indrek Sirkel and Pärtel Eelmere. Previous issues at gd.artun.ee/dearfriend

ALTERNATIVE EDUCATION SELF-ORGANIZED PRACTICES SUPPORTING COLLEAGUES PROLOGUES DIY TESTING

DEAR FRIEND,

You may have heard that I have finally started doing it—organizing an alternative educational platform for artists, designers and architects here in Estonia! It is called *proloogkool* (which loosely translates as "school of prologues")[1] and this thought (and name!) has been brewing inside my head for almost ten years now. But initiating something today seems much harder than years ago when things just happened in an ad hoc manner and I was more "in the mix"—co-running MÄRZ project space in Tallinn Old Town and researching self-organized practices for my PhD studies. As you know, I never finished my PhD, and after the building where our project space was located was sold to be turned into luxury apartments and fancy restaurants (one of those typical stories), I took a job as head of the Education Department in Kumu Art Museum and now as the head of the Centre for General Theory Subjects in the Estonian Academy of Arts.

But you know me. Besides my institutional job I have always had a second (voluntary/underpaid) job in a self-initiated art project in order to have more improvisational freedom and to be useful for the art community from different angles. I was itching for that—identifying small and specific gaps in how the art field here functions and proposing solutions. This means knowing your local pond well, being able to read the currents, having history and experience here accumulated over the years and through different positions. Gaps-hunting, yay!

The small art world here is operating with the same patterns as the larger cultural sector globally, corresponding to the demand to produce new (brilliant) ideas, works, situations in relentless rhythm, executing one project after another—or rather multiple projects at the same time. Meanwhile, on the local level there is a noticeable lack of public feedback (reflections, dialogues, interpretations, criticism) of exhibitions made, books published, events organized, etc. Probably tête-à-tête feedback is keeping the gears turning (along with the fun and purpose of doing those things), but still the feeling of loneliness is lurking behind the scenes. Small art fields tend to grow fragmented as you operate in multiple roles (¼ artist, ¼ organizer, ¼ lecturer, ¼ expert), with no critical mass to give its support to each of those roles. Everybody seems to be chronically busy and overbooked, entertaining the hope that cloning will be possible before burnout.

Taking into account all those deficiencies, what can be done? How can we support one another? How can we think along and give feedback, not just among our peer groups (and not just pushing art criticism)? We have that support during our BA or MA studies, but afterwards? And, outside this formal school system, how do we educate ourselves further? Most of us do systematic research when there is already an output format in place—an exhibition or book coming up, a public talk or lecture to give, etc. And we sporadically visit the "knowledge buffet" that is widely available in the form of podcasts and lectures, articles and books. But I think that very few of us have such superpowers that we are able to discipline ourselves independently during this knowledge-hunger quest, without external deadlines (that exhibition is about to open!) or commitments.

There was a trend in the 2000s in the contemporary art field to create educational platforms—big international art events, galleries, etc. declared themselves schools. It signalled, on the one side, a disappointment in the official educational system with its eroded values and increasing bureaucracy after Bologna reforms, and, on the other hand, a legacy of community arts, feminist educational groups, art-activism practices and relational aesthetics that resulted in the mainstream art world focusing their attention (and funds) on creating situations, not so much on artefacts. This never fully blossomed here in Estonia. There was a time when organizing reading groups and temporary learning spaces was more active, but more systematic experiments in creating hybrids of art and education didn't pick up. Now *proloogkool* has set the table and shared an open call inviting people to come along.

From September 2020 until June 2021, *proloogkool*'s first six participants and three mentors[2] are gathering once a month for a day. Between those meetings, participants are working with and researching their topic individually. To help them with structuring and time planning, designer Maria Muuk and I developed a special workbook for *proloogkool*. We are testing different formats with our meetings—presentations, group crit, individual longer meetings with mentors, exercises on writing, lectures-discussions about how to manage between multiple projects and how to find balance between your calling and taking time off. I have used *proloogkool* as an alibi to arrange meetings with participants and whomever they feel it would benefit them to meet. Collectively, we have reached the phase that requires inviting guests to develop our discussions further, so everyone made their wish list and voted. Balance between "being organized" and going with the flow is constantly being negotiated.

In a way, there is nothing new here. But new is not important (or exciting), while processing this shared space with actual people is. With so little fixed, the dynamics that are developing within this group is hard to communicate. What is it that we are actually doing? Perhaps creating a liminal space between colleagues and friends, professionalism and personal sphere? Thinking along. Getting and giving feedback on each other's ideas. Are the participants getting enough? We do not know yet, as we are in the middle. But I am already thinking that once a month is too sparse and that next year with the new group we should try to meet twice a month, to give more time and space for collective dynamics to develop. And I would love to discuss this temporary set of parallel prologue-schools with you, too! What are your experiences with self-organized education?

1. *http://proloogkool.eu/prologue-school-educational-programme* (only partly in English)

2. Anna Kaarma, Sille Kima, Piibe Kolka, Krista Mölder, Jane Remm and Mart Vainre; mentors Kai Lobjakas, Ingrid Ruudi and myself as a mentor-organizer.

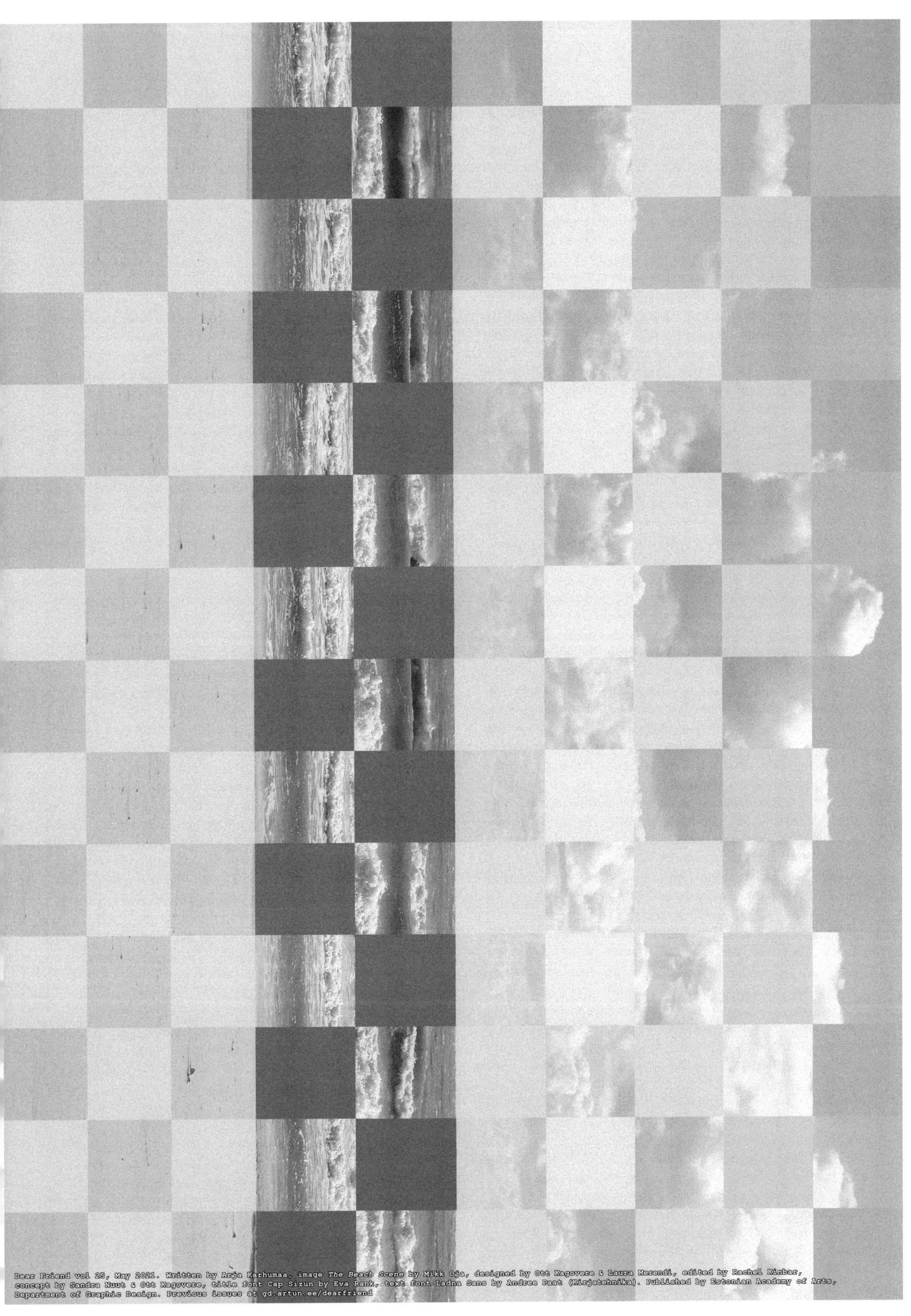

Dear Friend vol 25, May 2021. Written by Arja Karhumaa, image *The Beach Scene* by Mikk Oja, designed by Ott Kagovere & Laura Merendi, edited by Rachel Kinbar, concept by Sandra Nuut & Ott Kagovere, title font Cap Sizun by Eva Rank, text font Ladna Sans by Andree Paat (Kirjatehnika). Published by Estonian Academy of Arts, Department of Graphic Design. Previous issues at gd.artun.ee/dearfriend

IMAGINATION COGNITION DIAGRAMMATICS TYPOGRAPHY VISUAL EPISTEMOLOGY APHANTASIA

DEAR FRIEND,

I finally finished what I told you about—my doctoral thesis on design as writing. But much more than that happened, so much that I actually had to leave my most remarkable finding out of the thesis. It's rather personal and I want to share it with you, but where to start?

Like, did I ever tell you how I thought I hated Siri Hustvedt's novels? I just instinctively disliked them; they would trigger something that I failed to recognize. What frustrated me in particular was when Hustvedt describes completely fictional artworks by her imaginary artist characters, and yet she illustrates their most detailed features. The level of fabrication, fiction in fiction, vexes me, as it leaves me empty. Not to mention the description of dreams in fiction, don't get me started on that. I've been holding a grudge against descriptive writers throughout my adult life and have thrown books away in frustration. I couldn't find a reason for this. I shrugged it away, guessing it just wasn't my thing.

There were other clues, as well. A particular therapist was eager to use art therapy methods and sometimes put crayons in my hand. This always pained me: seriously, they give crayons to a designer and expect some primal expression? Trained to calculate and persuade by means of colour, form and texture, I was never able to drop that analytical armour. But more significantly: there was no colour in my mind, no mental image for my emotions. This became more evident when the same therapist wanted to do relaxation exercises where, guided by their voice, I was to walk on beaches and move through whatever spaces and landscapes. I didn't know how to tell them there was nothing, I was nowhere else than on my chair with my eyes closed. I felt like a failure. I was sure that I was just a control freak, unable to surrender to my own imagination.

I came across an article about aphantasia maybe three years ago. I passed it with a half-interested shrug: so that's a thing. Aphantasia is a feature where a person has no mental imagery, believed to be experienced by 3% of the population. A-phantasia: lack of fantasies. So there you have it. But I always considered myself so statistically average in my abilities, I never thought that had anything to do with me. It wasn't until I came across the same article a second time that I started reading it more closely, looking more closely, seeing—well, nothing but black. Previously, I had no words in my mind for not having images in my mind. Only now I realised that other people actually did.

Aphantasia. It feels overwhelming, and a little embarrassing, to say: it applies to me. I have lived 45 years of my life before realising how different my cognitive experience was compared to the statistically average person.

Do you have mental imagery? When I ask you to imagine a beach, do you see it? Is it a place you visited, or does it exist only in your imagination? And do you count sheep in order to trick yourself to sleep? I never understood that exercise when introduced to it as a child. I closed my eyes and looked for the sheep, but none ever came. I thought it was just some strange metaphor for counting: numbers as sheep. It never occurred to me I should literally see the sheep.

As I've realised I'm aphantasic, the shift in my reality is simultaneously non-existent and profound: everything is the same, but suddenly, I consider my mind, my imagination—this word I can never use neutrally again—from a new perspective, and re-evaluate the nature of my knowledge and the realm of my experience. So, nothing is the same. There is a world of mental imagery somewhere and I am not there and it is not in me.

Now it makes sense to me that I made a home out of text, writing, and typography. While reading, I cling to text and the materiality of language—the letters and spaces on the pages of the book. I never read visual descriptions of landscapes, people, or fictional works of art in order to construct them in my mind. Instead, I read to test the author's ability to write those into language, to encode them into strings of letters, to pursue in words what some fictional body perceives under their gaze. I tolerate descriptive language only if the language itself is carefully crafted, precise and eloquent.

I know you're already thinking this: my mind is not able to conjure a single image, still out of all professions I became a designer, professor and gatekeeper in visual communication design? You cannot miss the irony. All my life I told myself and others that I am a visual person, like when I used my "visual" memory in school exams—I was able to remember the location of the correct answer on the book page. But having read research on aphantasia I now understand this: a location is not an image. *What* and *where*, they are separate things, different realms in human cognition. I never had a mental image of the layout. Instead, I remembered what relations it consisted of. My mind works like a diagram, not a picture.

I used nine years of my life to slowly conduct a doctoral thesis about the material and diagrammatic aspects of text, trying to make sense of how language works spatially. I now realise I have unknowingly devoted my research to understanding the enigma of my own perception, why typography is so important for me. But now that I know what I know, I am less interested in my own experience than the implications this finding might have, and how I can take it forward. I have a feeling I am only beginning to understand the phenomena which Johanna Drucker has coined "visual epistemology" and "diagrammatic form". Because if *what* and *where* are different (although entangled) cognitive realms, might that have an impact on the way we do design?

And what is "visual", anyway? What if everything which we thought was just "visual" was something else too, all along?

Dear Friend vol 26, June 2021. Written by Rosen Eveleigh, image: "Our whispers intertwined" by Mikk Tanel Oja, designed by Ott Kagovere & Laura Merendi, edited by Rachel Kinbar, concept by Sandra Nuut & Ott Kagovere, title font Cap Sizun by Eva Rank, text font Ladna Sans by Andree Paat (Kirjatehnika). Published by Estonian Academy of Arts Department of Graphic Design. Previous issues at gd.artun.ee/dearfriend

DEAR FRIEND,

Cut to me: a spotlight illuminates an empty stage. I lean into the dust-glittered beam, huddling on the floor over a book cackling with unbridled glee. Who planted this here? Was this figure conjured up with the sole purpose to thrill to *me*?

Esther: 'If Kay had not existed, I might have had to invent her.'

Finding Esther and Kay happened just at the right time. I was several weeks into a residency high up in the Swiss mountains, where I was invited to work with a particularly uninteresting dead artist's library. I was doing nothing but getting over heartbreak. Morning coffee drunk whilst staring wistfully above the clouds forming across the neighbouring valley made the emotional drama all the more fabulous. It wasn't that I didn't feel like working. The library was simply too homophobic. Trans people and queers appeared within the pages of its books, but only as textbook pariahs: salacious criminals, medical illustrations of biological "freaks" or objects of heterosexual fantasy. I was struggling to joke myself out of these bad feelings, annoying myself with the question of what it might mean for me to point this out as part of the "work". Then I saw it. Wedged amongst the German men on the Philosophie II shelf: *Margaret Mead Made Me Gay*.

Margaret Mead Made Me Gay is a collection of writings by butch anthropologist heartthrob Esther Newton, charting her pioneering work on queer communities through personal and professional reflections. Tucked at the very end is an essay called "My Best Informant's Dress: The Erotic Equation in Fieldwork". Here lives Kay, a veteran resident of Cherry Grove, the long-standing queer haven located on Fire Island, who provides Esther with intel for her ethnographic research on the community.

When they meet, Kay is in her eighties and Esther in her thirties. When I meet them, Esther is in her eighties and I am in my thirties. Kay is a heartbreaker. A suave, wealthy, flirtatious, charming dyke who has both Esther and I crushing hard from the moment she rolls up on the boardwalk in her electric wheelchair, flashing her expensive dentures. So begins a 'pattern of flirtation and teasing' between the two, propelled by the possibility of fucking—their desire traversing erotic experience across histories. Kay, Esther, and me, are brought together in a three-way tryst and the thrill of legs touching under the table.

Esther: 'But now, instead of *having* ideas she *embodies* ideas. Kay spans almost the entire period from "smashing" and romantic friendship to the age of AIDS. When I kiss her I am kissing 1903.'

Esther confesses she probably wouldn't have fallen hook, line and sink-her for Kay had they met at the same age (because Kay's 'more of a party girl rather than an intellectual'). I'm not sure if their forms of lesbianism make them good boyfriend material for me either. If their forms of sexual legibility are interesting is it because it describes a path to mine, not a mirror image of it. Their relationship validates my own horny feelings, and how powerfully or honestly they might drive my work. I'm turned on by Kay, and by Esther being turned on by Kay. Our three-way flirtation grounds a basis of trust, and in turn, an ethics of research. A methodology for queer work.

Esther: 'My fieldwork experience has been fraught with sexual dangers and attractions that were much more like leitmotifs than light distractions.'

Perhaps I shouldn't admit I don't really like capital letters Graphic Design. I find it hard to muster enthusiasm for a certain design-guy reverence towards particular artefacts and their makers, materials, timestamps. Recipes of information blunt the affect of objects. Feelings, emotion and intimacy—too difficult to contain—become lost in favour of a simpler story. If the kind of design that floats my boat makes it into the canon, it can only be kept buoyant by holding onto my kind of erotics.

Sure, I'll confess I sometimes feel the thrill of a beautiful poster whilst scrolling myself into oblivion—but I've always feel a little cheap after giving it my like. I'm not interested in the aesthetics of design unless aestheticising cycles objectification back round to sociality. Instagram design might be hot if it were a real fetish, if variable type was a route to actualise bodily pleasure. But it's too disembodied for me. I'm busy thinking about Boyd McDonald jerking off on his single bed at Riverside Studios whilst compiling *Straight to Hell*, the proto queer zine that Boyd variably described as: 'The New York Review of Cocksucking', 'The American Journal of Revenge Therapy' or 'Just shameless, sorry'. I can't commit to the purely visual value of a poster and its accumulating status as air-conditioned archival *objet* when I'm drifting into a fantasy of how the bodies writhing together smelt in the darkness of the club night it was promoting. The poster is useful to the extent that it brought people to the club. I remember you would say nobody knows texts like designers do, that typesetting requires you to delicately stroke the end of every single line of text. (I'm trying to make a joke about ragging, but it seems I already have.)

The lesbian erotic photography book I've been working on for two years is wrapping up, and though it is my dream job I haven't got much to say about my *design decisions*. It's actually supposed to pass as a proper Art Book, so I played it straight. I mean, I hope it will be a beautiful book, but I don't care to claim that it's possible to see the conversations that went into making it. Only we know the ways in which it required us to turn around our identities like 3D renderings; how sometimes revelatory and other times disappointing it was to realise we were asking ourselves the same questions as the people in the images were asking 30 years ago. Our friends' and lovers' names litter its pages and will be printed 3,000 times and shipped to different parts of the world.

Whenever I open that InDesign document, the first face in the first photograph on the first page looks so much like yours I'm jolted across time to the year I was born. Suddenly, it is 1989 and I'm at the Castro Street Fair in San Francisco. A group of dykes wearing variations on leather and denim sit on top of a line of phone boxes, cutting a mid-line across the photograph. I catch them mid-euphoria, gassing and lighting each other's cigarettes, arms around each other and gesticulating a story. Every time, among the gazes, yours catches mine. In that moment we are held together. I give you a wink, and continue with my work.

ROSEN

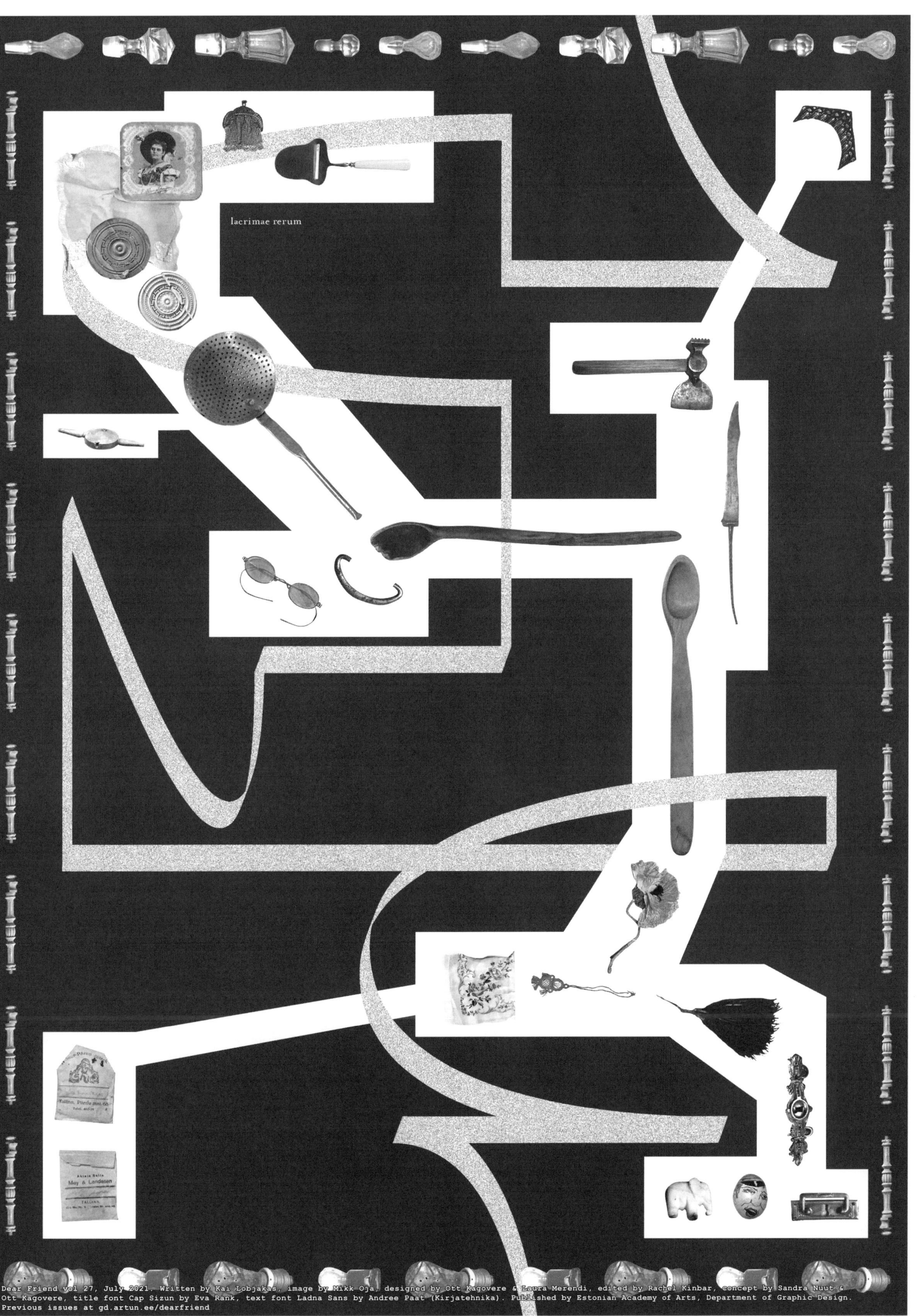

Dear Friend vol 27, July 2021. Written by Kai Lobjakas, image by Mikk Oja, designed by Ott Kagovere & Laura Merendi, edited by Rachel Kinbar, concept by Sandra Nuut & Ott Kagovere, title font Cap Sizun by Eva Rank, text font Ladna Sans by Andree Paat (Kirjatehnika). Published by Estonian Academy of Arts, Department of Graphic Design. Previous issues at gd.artun.ee/dearfriend

COLLECTING CONTEMPLATING TEARS OF THINGS RANDOMNESS FRAGMENTS ENCAPSULATION

DEAR FRIEND,

In a situation where suddenly so much of the ordinary froze and disappeared, I actually enjoyed the randomness it brought and the fact that there was time. I took pleasure in the possibility of spending time at home that I believe many, including me, often lack. Even the movement of light throughout the day is experiential. Naturally and soon enough, it was evident that the fun factor present in many activities—even the ordinary pre- and post-talks at meetings—was missing.

I have never before had to so often answer questions about the origins of objects or practice one of the favorite parts of my work—making home visits. The immediate surroundings, details of the everyday environment were discovered, possessions reorgnised and re-evaluated. New collections were initiated and older collections changed owners. A significant number of new collectors emerged. The prices of certain objects have risen to unprecedented heights. Statistics from the local central auction portal reveal the unseen numbers both in queries and deals. Considering how the past is coded in our future, this kind of relating seems to help people come to terms with their past. Collecting is done with a certain unsentimental nostalgia.

My activities have long been accompanied by a continuous relation to the old, history, brushing things out from the past. I have been engaged in looking for and finding objects, memories, materials—and it suits me well. I have developed a sharpened sense and fine-tuned instinct for making observations, but also a certain kind of positive numbness that allows me occasionally to ignore. I have always been pleased that my work allows me to be relatively free from the urge to build a personal collection.

For a while now I've been eager to write you about something that started approximately a year ago and has continued for some time.

One day last spring I was standing in an old house soon to be sold that was filled with fragments from several generations. The only rational aspect in the house was that most of the older material was buried and the newer layers covered the previous. So, I was in the middle of these micro-worlds that were awaiting their destiny—to be packed or given up—depending on my expert verdict.

On one hand, these were some of the most exciting things I have seen, but on the other it was a distressing amount of everyday materials: all the letters and postcards from decades ago that noone ever rereads, opera programs from visiting Vienna, Berlin and other European cities in the 1920s with tickets between the pages, receipts of things and services consumed, turned fragments of chairs, old clothing kept for the value of the material, lace collars, tablecloths featuring Richelieu embroidery, a measuring stick with the old metric system, plugs from lost or broken carafes, glass, metal, bone and wooden walking sticks, vases and stationery, neo-renaissance, functionalist, rattan and tubular steel furniture, a desk ventilator, a fully packed bag for fishing, faience and porcelain tableware, glass and crystal goblets, cutlery, ceramic doll heads, brass bras, decorative lock-plates and handles, marble elephants, a packet of anemone seeds from 1931, jewelry, candy and cigarette boxes, paper and bamboo Japanese parasols, artificial flowers, unfinished and beaded embroidery, silk shawls, handkerchiefs with lace details and monogrammed boxes, lamp shades, powdered sulfur in a carefully folded paper cover, spices, essences, books about engineering, medicine and religious studies, fragments of memoirs, medicine in apothecary packaging, copper vessels, cast iron pans, a travel clock in a leather case, hundreds of keys, a butterfly collection, empty Champagne and wine bottles kept in the pantry under the staircase, rusty cake and biscuit forms, board games, lighting chains with sharp-ended bulbs. All juicy snippets of past lives, new and old objects and collections holding meaning. It was the most organic way of these things being together.

I was anxious about everything that might fall apart, and I had never stumbled upon such an amount and variety of things. Every layer took me by surprise. Typologies of objects, habits and possibilities of people, mentalities, determination, respect of the past and concern for the future unfolded. Never before have I felt so perplexed and helpless among things. It outweighs the heaviness of the systematically collected material and provides so much to contemplate, like the people who had lived there but also how to handle the encapsulated hints of lifestyle, habits and customs that accumulated in such a natural manner.

So we packed almost a houseful of pieces and took them to a safe place to have some time to contemplate them, browse the fragments of memoirs, draw connections.

During the whole process I was thinking about the first book from Edmund de Waal, which I basically swallowed ten years ago. It was an enchanting historical story about tracking the origin of the netsuke collection his family possessed. A reconstruction of family history, heritage, expropriation of the property during the Second Word War and wider relations to cultural history. It was a narrative running through materiality and objects, creating beautiful connections with people and their ties to the everyday world describing (among other issues) the *lacrimae rerum*, tears of things.

When I had more or less finished this letter, I received a new book by de Waal, "Letters to Camondo", in which he sort of continues reconstructing the family history. He focuses on a distant relative's neighbor, Moïse de Camondo, whose spectacular house on rue de Monceau in Paris was filled with 18th century French paintings and was to be inherited by his son Nissim who sadly was killed in the First World War and so the house was bequeathed to the French state in his honor. Currently there's a museum that has stayed untouched since 1936. The book consists of imaginary letters to the count, and this time the preface reads "*lacrimae rerum*" and chapters begin with the phrase "Dear friend!" and continuing at the very beginning: "As you may have guessed by now, I am not in your house by accident."

So, these are the things that keep me going these days.

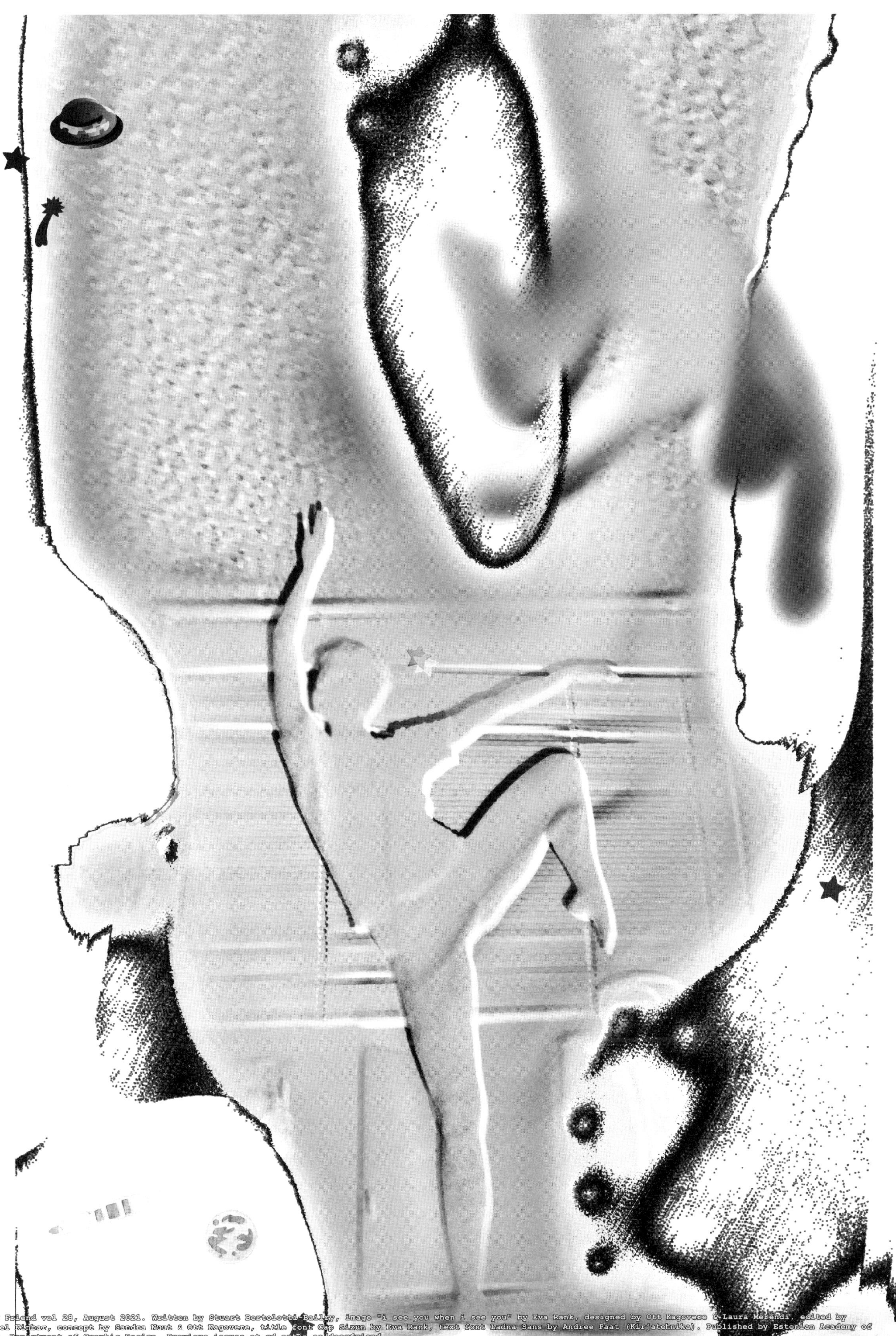

Dear Friend vol 28, August 2021. Written by Stuart Bertolotti-Bailey, image "i see you when i see you" by Eva Rank, designed by Ott Kagovere & Laura Merendi, edited by Rachel Kinbar, concept by Sandra Nuut & Ott Kagovere, title font Cap Sizun by Eva Rank, text font Ladna Sans by Andree Paat (Kirjatehnika). Published by Estonian Academy of Arts, Department of Graphic Design. Previous issues at gd.artun.ee/dearfriend

OPTICAL ILLUSION LOCKDOWN PROJECT PRISON TEMPLATE EITHER/OR THE SHAWSHANK REDEMPTION

DEAR FRIEND,

Shortly after the first lockdown began some fifteen months or so ago, the Institute of Contemporary Arts in London where I work began releasing an 'ICA Daily' email—being a scattershot list of online viewing, reading and listening compiled at speed by our curators and promptly dispatched at 10am every morning, including weekends.

When I first overhauled the ICA's graphic identity back in 2017, one ingredient of the DNA was a set of 'classic' optical illusions, such as the well-known Duck-Rabbit, Impossible Triangle, or Reversible Stairs. The idea was to put these images to work as visual headers for categories that didn't otherwise have any obvious title or unifying theme. Many of these illusions have an 'either/or' aspect, in the sense that the Duck-Rabbit is both duck *and* rabbit. They are fundamentally difficult to pin down and, as such, usefully ambiguous—as optical *allusions*. They also have the benefit of being free-floating, freely signifying icons that don't really belong to anyone, surely doing the rounds in the public domain long before intellectual property or copyright laws were dreamed up.

As time went on, we started to use the illusions more broadly to represent—or avoid representing—various bits and pieces of the Institute. I keep a folder of unused examples on my desktop waiting to be summoned for use, and, when the idea of the daily email came up, the illusion of Eternal Stairs most famously depitcted in M.C. Escher's 1960 lithograph 'Ascending and Descending' seemed perfectly suited: a series of quotidian steps of unknown duration or destination, operating outside any regular sense of time and space. To emphasise the ennui, I animated the staircase by highlighting each subsequent step with a yellow panel, plodding round and round and round and round.

With this image in mind, and against my better instincts, I thought I'd take this opportunity to highlight another couple of Lockdown Projects that caught my attention. I say 'against my better instincts' because I consider myself the opposite of a lockdown project sort of person—and in fact I only happened across the first one thanks to the headline 'I Don't Want to See Your Quarantine "Art" Unless It's This'.

It was an attempt by members of two London-based bands, Fat White Family and Pregoblin, to re-enact the entirety of the 1994 'cult mainstream' film *The Shawshank Redemption* scene by scene on Instagram Stories. What appealed to me above all was how the two groups' vocalists, Lias Saoudi and Alex Sebley—who respectively play the Morgan Freeman and Tim Robbins roles—seemed to be taking such a ridiculous idea so seriously, or at least were attempting to do it with some degree of rigour and commitment, whatever that might have meant at the beginning of the first wave of Covid.

Naturally, it all takes place within the confines of what is presumably one of their houses, starting out in a shabby garden (prison yard), then moving into a sparsely populated lounge (prison cell) while swigging freely from cans of beer (cups of water). The only piece of the fictional fourth wall left remotely intact, in fact, is their risky yet plausible attempt to mimic the two characters' American accents.

I've long forgotten the source of a phrase I once read or heard that describes good design work as 'carrying the right weight'—which I take to mean an equilibrium between form and content, or vehicle and material. And in the case of this Insta-Shawshank, there's something about the bare bones of an epic Hollywood script being squeezed through the severely restrictive possibilities of a social media channel within our newly claustrophobic Covid World that carries the right weight for me. Or maybe it's just the dumb idea of a prison film being made from the prison of lockdown that seems oddly liberating. To my considerable disappointment, they only made it as far as three scenes before apparently giving up.

My other highlight also takes the form of an incremental series, though this one is still apparently ongoing at the time of writing. Richard Dawson is a beloved, difficult-to-summarize musician from Newcastle who released a masterpiece single of very English social realism called 'Jogging' in 2019, soon followed by the album '2020' just months before the year in question became a write-off.

On the very first day of the first UK lockdown, Monday March 23, Dawson and his bandmate/partner Sally Pilkington quietly issued a 10-minute piece of hypnotic, lo-fi ambient music via Bandcamp under the name Bulbils, and continued to release an extended piece or suite of similar music on a daily basis. The individual tracks are mostly named by a single word ('Funnel', 'Mole', 'Oxygen') then collected under a similarly blank or deadpan umbrella title ('Donkey', 'Mounds', 'Spring'), gradually becoming more suggestive ('Child's Dreaming of a Storm', 'The Palace at Day and Night', 'Journey of the Canada Goose') and even vaguely topical ('Conspiracy Faeries', 'Tax Return', 'Vaccine') as the weeks and months roll on.

There's a resounding graphic design note to the project too, as each release comes with its own little square of artwork based on a simple template: 1. a suggestible image, as loosely related to the title as the titles are to the music, and 2. the word 'Bulbils' set in some strangely specific font in the top left corner.

Writing this now, I realize that what I really love about the project is precisely how slippery the whole thing is. The music + the title + the image + the typeface *almost* amount to a meaningful whole. But not quite. At times Bulbils feels like a joke or pastiche, at others like a form of therapy or coping mechanism. And like those optical illusions, it doesn't have to be one thing or the other. It can also be neither or both or all of the above.

In these two projects—one outlandish, one meditative—I can dimly perceive an alignment of the form and content *of the Pandemic itself* that have intermittently nourished me while regular culture has been on hold.

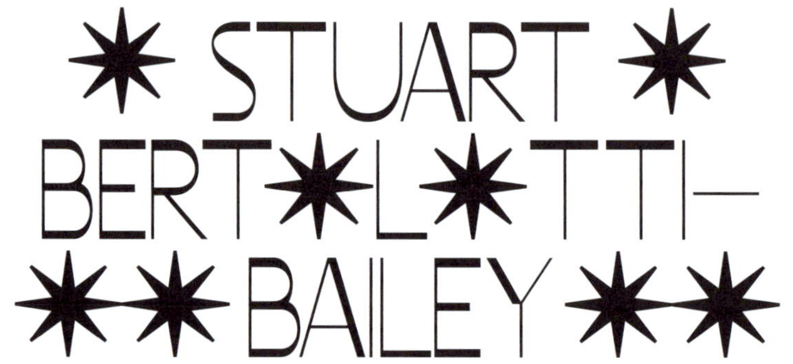

Better an 'oops' than a 'what if'

Dear Friend vol 29, September 2021. Written by Alice Twemlow, image by Eva Rank, designed by Ott Kagovere & Rainer Kasekivi, edited by Rachel Kinbar, concept by Sandra Nuut & Ott Kagovere, title font Cap Sizun by Eva Rank, text font Ladna Sans by Andree Paat (Kirjatehnika). Thank you: Estonian Academy of Arts, Department of Graphic Design.
Previous issues at gd.artun.ee/dearfriend

ENVIRONMENTAL HUMANITIES CLIMATE IMAGINARIES LITERARY ECO-FICTION POST-DESIGN BREAK-UP LETTER

DEAR FRIEND,

Because that's what we are, right? I know others seemed to think it was more than that, but if we're honest, we were never truly *passionate.* Sure, we looked good together at exhibition openings. Our forms fit. But for what purpose? At first, we found it (ironically) thrilling that we subscribed to the same magazines and, later, podcasts; that we had matching Ally Capellino cross-body bags; and could cross reference our icon pilgrimage checklists—Marfa, Therme Vals, Lightning Field, Dessau... We were mutually affectionate desk mates, international conference chums. We spoke the same images, tasted the same letterspacing, heard the same textures. We knew what was good, what was so bad it was good, and everything else in between.

Time passed like this. Almost four decades in fact. And the next thing we knew, I had begun to feel differently about you and you had begun... well, these days I don't presume to know what you think. You may well have a whole other version of events: you taught me everything I know; we shared *context*, for gods' sake; I'm ungrateful and a betrayer.

Ok, I have to admit that writing this down is making me nervous. What if you do freak out and block me on social media, air me IRL? Worse still, what if you don't even notice I've gone? I know I'm the one who thinks we should see other people, but what if I change my mind later? I mean, we've been through so much together. What if, after I forsake your form, I don't have any function? What if, after I strip away your skin, I don't have any content?

I was only 9 or 10 when I figured out who you were. That what my Dad did for work, and the Milton Glaser posters on our walls and the speckled blue enamel mugs as pen pots, my doodling in Cooper Black on my schoolbooks, was all part of it. Of you. Since then, I've put in the hours to get to know you better and I've got the column inches, the archival record request receipts, and the letters after my name to prove it. I wrote the questions, transcribed the stories; I problematized the assumptions, unpacked the concepts, cited the sources; I pored over the halftones, picas, pixels; clicked the links, smelt the ink, revered the gradient, stroked the grain, put my cheek to the cool ceramic, snagged my tights on the composite, paced the perimeter, checked to see if the green roof Sempervivum was being watered...

We've called each other different names, as it suited us. In the bylines, I was your historian, commentator, biographer, critic, curator, and your progeny's educator. You were my visual culture, manmade environment, material culture. At times you were pretty much everything that took shape for a reason from a plan. Sometimes you wanted me to be your stage-door groupie and I gladly bore your autograph below my collar bone. Other times you wanted me to be your mother and I folded my words around you and held you tight. Then you got serious and wanted me to nominate you for club membership, to lobby for you, to lend you academic rigor, disciplinary validation. Remember that time you thought you wanted me to be your moral conscience? Well, that was awkward.

You used me. But I used you right back. I needed you to be my muse, my subject, but also my atmosphere, my filter. I'm looking at my bookshelf right now and it's filled with you. I'm looking out the window and the whole street is you.

So what went wrong? It wasn't you, it was... but then again, it was *you* who made all those things. Beautiful, sleek, useful, novel, helpful, cheerful, disposable and, ultimately, indelible. But I didn't protest. Far from it. It was *me* who helped you hawk your yarns, spin your wares. Embedded, compromised, critically intimate, I took sensory pleasure in the wrapping and the unboxing, the consuming and the throwing away.

Ah, the throwing away. Took me a while, but when I realized there was no *away*, just displacement, well that's where things really began to fall apart for us wasn't it. Our phone began to leach its persistent bioaccumulative toxins into rivers and bloodstreams; the laminate we specified for that bookcover grew up to be a lump of anthro-geo-monster-moltenglomerate, the planet's newest rock form; our kid's fleece, so convenient, wore down into millions of microfibers and, with a flush, fed the fishies; our digital profligacy, the backups, abandoned folders and websites, were kept, it turned out, not in a fluffy cloud, as advertised, but in a heavy, energy consuming millstone. Each night, when I said I was tired, it was because I was reckoning all the ways in which the material fallout from our agile, smart, creative industry was being irreversibly laid down in the planetary strata, condensed in the atmospheric record, concentrated in our biological legacies, and trophic-transferred via a diminishing range of species to our deep futures. Here was a plan in which I didn't want a part, an archive in which I didn't want to linger. Tired? We're exhausted.

And even when I began to smell the black-boxed, aluminum-brand-capsule coffee maker, I still stayed. If anyone can mop up its own mess, it's you, I thought. Look at all these critically intervening green walls, circular diagrams, refillable bottles, biodegradable straws, tote bags, tool libraries, kelp sneakers, mycelium chairs, recycled plastic hair combs...

Give me a break. Give me some distance. Actually, about that... I know I told you my bags are packed and ticket is booked. And it's true I'm going away, but I'm also staying right here.

I used to try and bring fiction to you. I gave you biographies, ideal careers, afterlives, even deviant agency. But you never read them. So now I'm going to fiction. They've made room for me in their shared workspace. And you're going back to the background. You'll be there, but only in the service of character—resting on tabletops and reclining in pockets, waiting for your cue to be coveted, polished, repaired, stolen, hugged or thrown away. But not for real this time. In fiction, you are, on the whole, much less harmful.

So I guess that's it. I hope you will come and visit once I've settled in.

I'm leaving my key but taking the memories... sorry, not sorry. Oh, and the fish has been fed.

Yours,

Dear Friend vol 31, November 2021. Written by Saara Hannus, image by Martina Gofman, designed by Ott Kagovere & Rainer Kasekivi, edited by Rachel Kinbar, concept by Sandra Nuut & Ott Kagovere, title font Cap Sizun by Eva Rank, text font Ladna Sans by Andree Paat (Kirjatehnika). Thank you Estonian Academy of Arts, Department of Graphic Design. Previous issues at gd.artun.ee/dearfriend

FEELINGS

ATTACHMENT

KISSES

CONNECTION

** DEAR FRIEND,

I wonder what you're doing now. I wonder if you're somewhere kissing someone, or looking into someone's eyes, maybe talking about art or love.

I kissed someone yesterday. We had been walking along the coastline of the city and sitting at the corner table of a neighborhood pub until it closed. We were standing awkwardly on the street saying goodbyes. After some seconds of silence they asked if we should kiss, and I replied: *Do you mean now?* I have no idea why I said that. So awkward! Maybe I was nervous about taking that step, even though I knew we should just decide to do it. I realised I should say yes and said it and leaned on them and they leaned back and our lips touched. They were probably feeling nervous too, because their lips were a bit tight. I believe my lips were quite soft and moist, haha, at least I hope so. I love soft lips.

It was scary to kiss, and I think I was counting seconds rather than being in the moment, but I felt relieved afterwards. I don't know what'll happen with this person, but I reckon in a dating context it's good to kiss as soon as possible, just to test how it feels. But first kisses are never too good, are they? Do you remember your best first kisses? I don't. I just like it if they last looooooong and get better every second. Every kiss is a new chance for a better kiss. Getting to know someone by kissing is great!

I wonder if you feel your lips with your tongue or teeth when you paint. I wonder if you imagine moving your tongue on the canvas. I'm thinking of that piece you painted with your whole body, "made love" to the painting, and the painting was "making love". I'm using quotation marks because I feel a bit weird using the expression "making love". I think sex is something other than an act of love—it's an act of enjoyment and play and mutual exploration. But I remember you talking about making love when talking about the work, and I was left thinking about the love we have for our work. I'm thinking we both really love our work.

Many of the artists I know are kind of *married* to their work. They have an intense (maybe even pretty toxic?) relationship with their practice. They dive so deep into it that human relationships can never reach those depths. I'm not as invested in my work as I am in my romantic relationships. I'm always thinking of desire and crushes and interpersonal dynamics and feelings and commitment in relationships, and when I work I make art about those processes too. But I guess if my work focuses on those topics, then I'm working almost all the time, haha (well, who isn't these days).

Would be interesting to know what you've been reading lately. I recently finished Jessica Fern's *Polysecure*, and I totally recommend it if you're at all interested in attachment theory. It's basically about how our attachment styles affect our relationships and how we can navigate loving relationships with a sense of security, specifically in the context of nonmonogamy. If you're not familiar with the concept, attachment styles are formulations that help us understand how our previous emotional experiences influence our relationships. Attachment theory is usually centered in very early childhood, focusing on the impact made by our relationship with our primary caregiver, but Fern highlights the influence of other local communities and culture as well with a "nested model of attachment and trauma". For me, as a queer person, it's been interesting to think about the feeling of not fitting into society's norms, about the experience of being an outsider, and how that experience has affected my attachment behaviour.

The book introduced a thought about attachment I was super excited about: that one could kinda decide one's attachment figures, the people you have an attachment bond with. I realised I always sought attachment whenever I had feelings for someone, and it usually led to heartbreak. So I wanted to test it out. I was seeing someone and told them I had previously been quite anxiously attached to people I had fallen for, but wanted to try to be more conscious about my attachment. I told them I planned to ask for availability for an attachment bond. They said: *But isn't it a bit too late to ask if you already have feelings for someone?* I said I didn't know but wanted to try. It failed completely. My preoccupied attachment started coming to the surface as soon as I developed feelings. They didn't want anything serious and I couldn't do casual, as I was already fiercely seeking an attachment bond with them, meaning I expected them to be available, responsive and emotionally engaged, when in fact they weren't. I got burned once again. :(Yeah, so I don't suggest trying that. I've come to the conclusion I don't really understand what *casual* means in terms of relationships. Is it about not having feelings? TELL MEEEEEE

My friend just posted a "spiritual journey" quote on Instagram saying something like we shouldn't get attached to the people or things we love, but instead "let beautiful connections pass through without attachment". I keep coming back to that thought, over and over again, realizing I haven't been practicing that. I think in the realm of work it's easier to love freely. Like after our studio visit, I felt a nice connection with you but didn't feel the need to be in constant contact with you. I trusted our conversation and connection would continue and keep growing over time without forcing it. I hope you feel the same way.

Anyway, thanks for reading. Would love to hear your thoughts if you have time to write back.

WITH LOVE, AS ALWAYS,
SAARA HANNUS

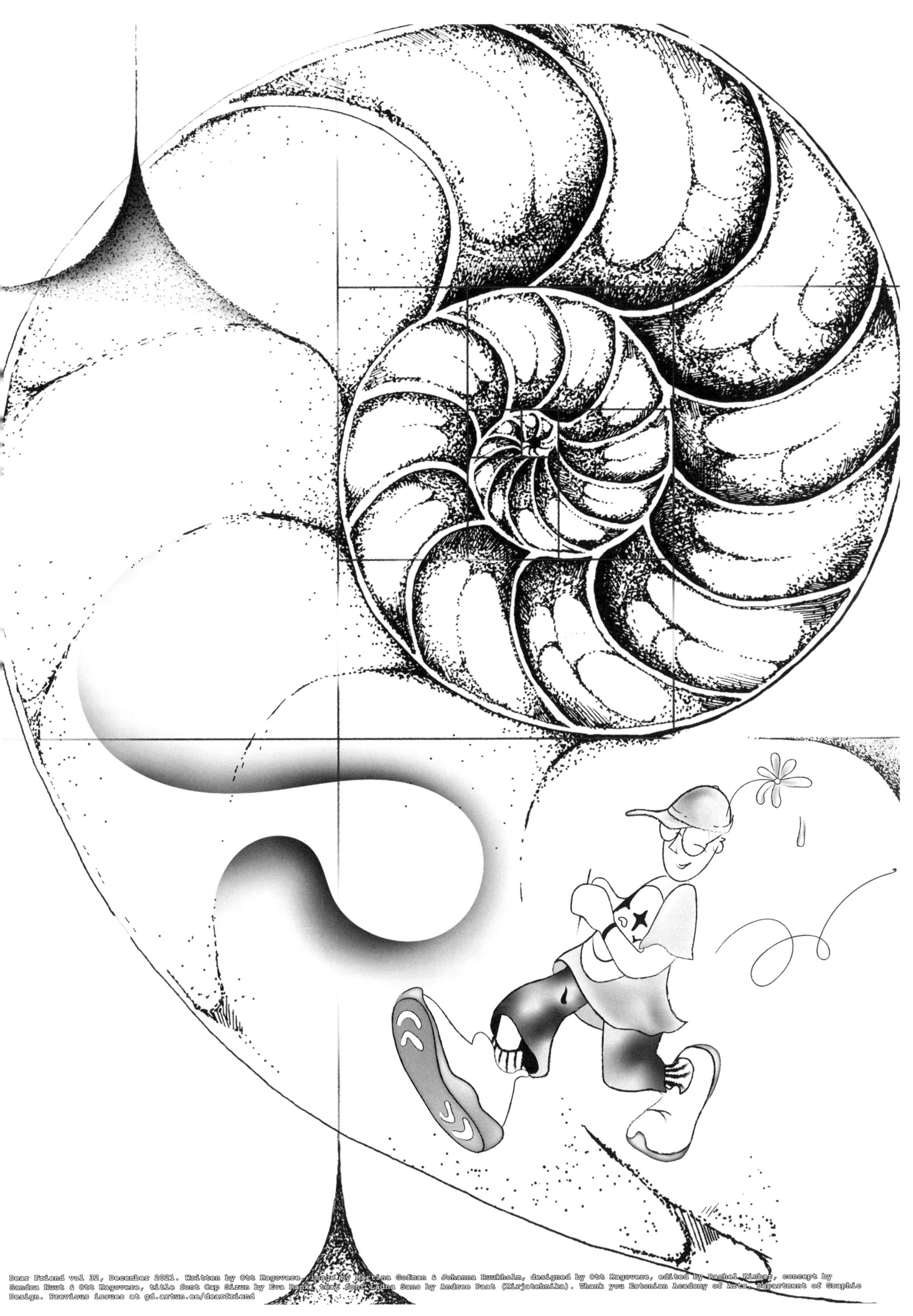

Dear Friend vol 32, December 2021. Written by Ott Kagovere, image by Martina Gofman & Johanna Ruukholm, designed by Ott Kagovere, edited by Rachel Kinbar, concept by Sandra Nuut & Ott Kagovere, title font Cap Sizun by Eva Rank, text font Ladna Sans by Andree Paat (Kirjatehnika). Thank you Estonian Academy of Arts, Department of Graphic Design. Previous issues at gd.artun.ee/dearfriend

CLEANING

WRITING

SOLID ARGUMENTS

SISYPHOS

BROOM

DEAR FRIEND,

I know there's much to catch up on, but I really want to talk to you about cleaning. In a funny way, I have been obsessed with it lately. I haven't actually been cleaning much, but I have been thinking about it a lot while doing some other things. Usually we tend to procrastinate by cleaning, but for me fantasizing about it is quite enough.

I thought about it a lot while writing this letter. I was constantly lost in thought, constructing sentences in my mind, while staring around with a blank gaze. My room is a bit of a mess, so I guess it's no surprise that the allusion of cleaning was constantly popping up. Soon enough this mess started to provide me with several metaphors and storylines to hang on to until I reached a conclusion that writing and cleaning are essentially the same.

Here are my arguments for it:

1. BOTH ARE OFTEN DONE WITH A CERTAIN AUDIENCE IN MIND

I always clean the best when someone is coming over and the same goes in writing—it's always easier when you have a certain audience in mind. Even if the audience is very private—perhaps a personal diary meant for my eyes only—it is still written as if it was meant for someone else. I guess it relies on the fact that we are alien to ourselves, as well. I am sure this is the reason why we are always surprised about the stuff that we write and often feel detached from the writing when it's done. It is as if the text belongs to someone else. But in reality I don't think the texts belong to anyone. They are their own subjects. The moment a text is published it enters the public sphere, meaning it belongs to everyone engaging with it, not someone in particular.

If we compare this to cleaning, then it becomes apparent that a reader of a text is nothing but a guest in our head. When they come over, the least we can do is make up our mind, change the sheets like a white page, and show some hospitality by constructing a temporary order in thought.

Cleaning also has that element of surprise that makes writing so rewarding. I often find the strangest things under the sofa or behind the bookshelf. I once found an old pencil, a green one, hidden behind a desk. I think I remember buying it when I was 18. It still works, and every time I use it for writing or drawing it fills me with vague memories of adolescence.

2. CLEANING IS ALWAYS TEMPORARY AND SO IS WRITING

I really think that if Sisyphus had been given a broom to sweep the hills instead of pushing a boulder over them, he would have learned the same lesson. It would have been even better if the gods had given him a pen and a paper and cursed him to write every day. In that case I would really see Sisyphus as a writer like Thomas Bernhard[1]—who seems to be writing the same novel over and over again.

For him, writing is clearly a boulder to be pushed from book to book. In that sense it almost does not matter what he writes about. In *Concrete* we are not interested in his obsessive loathing of his "fictional" sister, or in *The Loser* the constant repetition of the genius of Glenn Gould and the crushing smallness of other characters. In his novels we are not looking for a resolution to the events happening. Instead, what fascinates us is the sisyphean struggle that Bernhard faces while writing. A struggle that is present from sentence to sentence, chapter to chapter, and book to book. It is the same struggle that Camus calls the absurdity of life in his *The Myth of Sisyphus* and which manifests itself in writing through the fact that we are constantly trying to communicate but language only meets us halfway.

The same rule applies to cleaning. No matter how thorough and precise you are, you still have to pick up the broom again sooner or later. In that sense, a clean room is very similar to a well-phrased sentence. When everything is in its "right" place, either in a text or in a living room; it always becomes a peculiar *mise en scene*, an extremely slow piece of art, that pats us on our back and tells us to try again.

To come back to Camus, I really agree with him that the never ending task of Sisyphus makes him happy. One can see the limitations of our language as a burden. But for me it takes the pressure off from writing, because there is always a second chance, always enough language to push around like a boulder.

3. A THIRD ARGUMENT!

For the sake of good structure and good taste a third argument for writing and cleaning should be presented here in an elegant fashion. Written with great passion and admirable rigour. If I remember correctly, this advice was given in 1637 by Rene Descartes in his *Discourse on Method*. He was certain that a good essay presents three ideas and never more, because the reader is incapable of digesting more information at once.

I am not really a student of Descartes, but somehow for this particular letter having a third "argument" kind of makes sense. Even though it is just a formal one, it makes this text feel complete. Makes it sound as if we would be playing a harmonic chord. It looks trustworthy from afar and while reading it has a logical ending. So without further adieu, I sincerely thank you for reading and hope to hear from you soon!

1. Thomas Bernhard (1931–1989) was an Austrian writer, and I would really recommend his books to you if you are not already into them. In the context of letter writing, I would like to point out that his novels are basically extremely long letters consisting of obsessive inner monologues. I know I know, such are the worst letters to receive, but surprisingly they make a great novel!

SANDRA NUUT
**
PAUL SOULELLIS
**
JACK SELF
**
CLAUDIA DOMS
**
EIK HERMANN
**
MARYAM FANNI
**

INDREK SIRKEL
**
MAARJA KANGRO
**
NELL DONKERS
**
SEAN YENDRYS
**
RACHEL KINBAR
**
OTT KAGOVERE
**

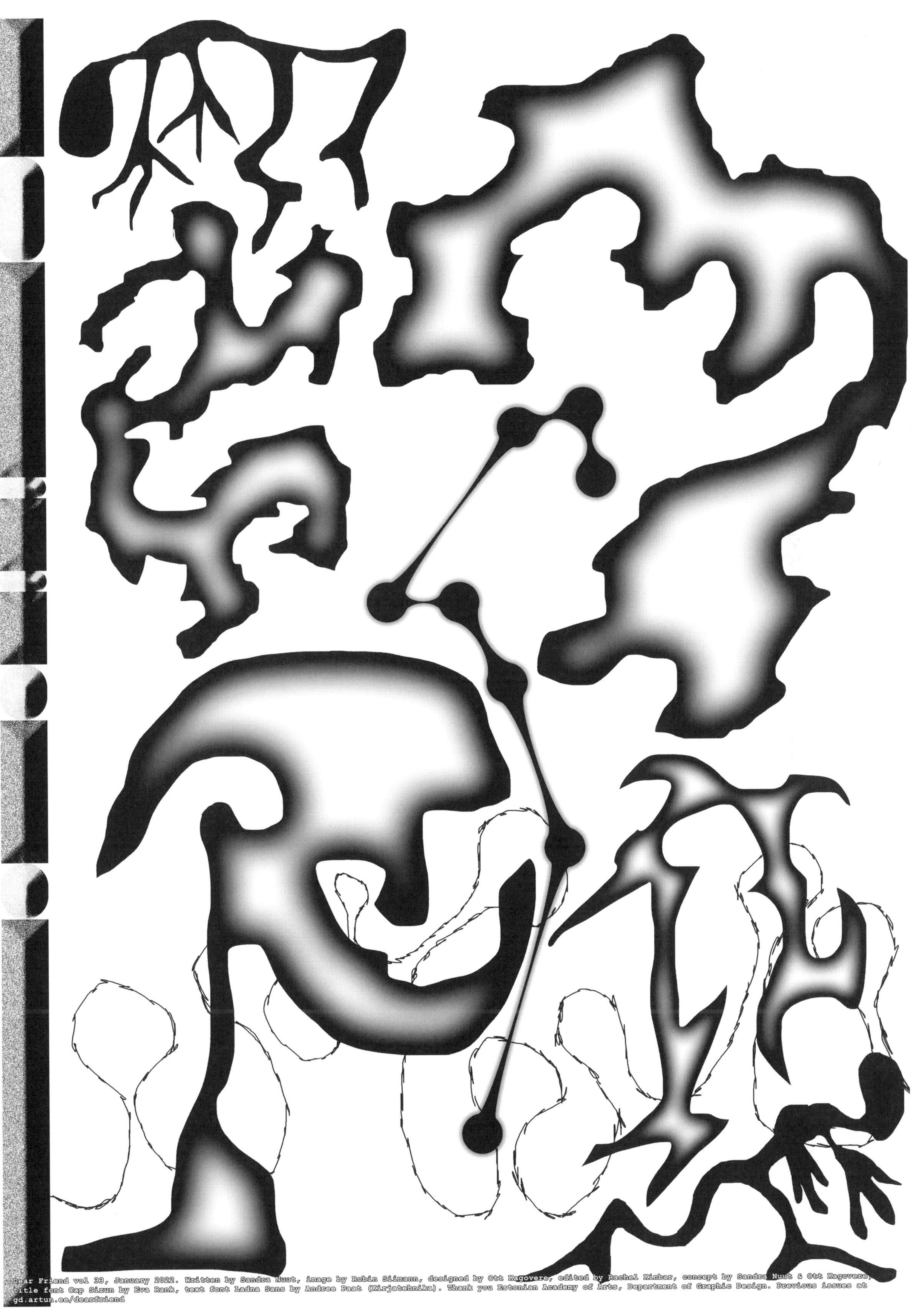

Dear Friend vol 33, January 2022. Written by Sandra Nuut, image by Robin Siimann, designed by Ott Kagovere, edited by Rachel Kinbar, concept by Sandra Nuut & Ott Kagovere, title font Cap Sizun by Eva Rank, text font Ladna Sans by Andree Paat (Kirjatehnika). Thank you Estonian Academy of Arts, Department of Graphic Design. Previous issues at gd.artun.ee/dearfriend

ACCIDENTAL

TEACHING & LEARNING

BELL HOOKS

WELLBEING

EDUCATION

DEAR FRIEND,

I have been thinking about you these past weeks while taking a course for university teachers, reading a book by the late bell hooks, and grading papers. Somehow 2022 has started strong on an academic note. I guess I am a teacher. I never planned it. Mentioning the lecturer title still makes my stomach squeeze, although I have thrown myself into it all. The very beginning of working at the art academy was rather accidental and—let me be honest—a way to safely return to the motherland. This does not mean that I was not interested. I told you back then that I was keen. I wanted to teach and somehow thought that it provides time for reflection. This was a bit blue-eyed of me but it has provided this and, strangely enough, changed me as a human being.

This temporary phase in education has grown into about five years so far. The first year was full of events for which I was never prepared for professionally, pedagogically, psychologically... I hope that enough time has passed to mention the trauma of seeing someone performing their first performance while intentionally harming themselves physically... or responding to aggressive student emails about what the staff was doing wrong. These are some wild interactions engraved in my memory as they welcomed me into this academic life. I felt I was in the middle, trying to navigate between students and administration and found a chasm between it all. Somehow these major issues resolved themselves to some extent, and possibly something larger was pushed into the process after these and some other events as today there is an ethical code and committee.

Younger teachers ask questions once or twice every semester that relate to students' wellbeing, and these bring back the memory of that first year. We are calmer these days. I hope this calmness does not offend you. We care. There is some experience, yet there is a lot to do in terms of preparing us to respond to mental health questions, learning difficulties, next to trying to do a good lecture or engaging seminar, which is also not something that happens easily. Sometimes it does not happen. My dear colleague said that teaching is where one day you are feeling on top, that it flows and you might be thinking that you are starting to get it, and then the next day you are reminded with a kick in the ass that no, it is not so easily achievable. The word humility starts to look and sound different. We are teaching and learning, as they say, and although students need our support, they also want us to challenge them. It sounds like writer bell hooks sits among us: "They want and demand more from professors than my generation did. There are times when I walk into classrooms overflowing with students who feel terribly wounded in their psyche (many of them see therapists), yet I do not think that they want therapy from me. They do want an education that is healing to the uninformed, unknowing spirit. They do want knowledge that is meaningful."* Preparing courses makes the reality both messy and exciting. There is no lecture or course that I can pull out of my sleeve or refer to my good old memory, let alone think of healing anyone. I sit with the books, reading and researching to understand the things that I plan to share until late hours. It probably shows but that is where I am, growing together with you, navigating the worlds of education, design history, pedagogy, and more, and then back to the classroom.

One of the interesting aspects is our age gap. It is not that big, although it is indeed growing every year. What I am learning and seeing is the fabric of the next generation. I wish I had a similar experience with older generations, a chance to understand them as a collective. The young today that I see are braver, more worldly, open, self-confident, demanding than we ever were with our teachers (or at least than I was). I wish I had called out a lecturer about not providing any titles with hundreds of artworks that she was clicking through in a minute on a slide projector and expecting us to memorize it all, or another teacher making remarks about someone's low intelligence. It was not all bad, not at all, but I see that some young teachers challenge themselves more. They want to reach the student and not only bathe in their own knowledge. Education as it seems is not only sharing facts and ideas, but connecting through the field that we are both interested in. I cannot say that I manage any of my expectations and can only promise that they are there.

I have also noticed that I was privileged to have had the time to be young—to make mistakes and explore—during my studies. I don't think this is the case often right now. Most of our younger students work one or two jobs next to a full-time program. Last year in a seminar where we discussed neoliberalism and its effects on art education, one student mentioned that her dream is to have a place to live, food, and a fine job. It was beautiful and sad at once. None of their dreams sounded as grand and utopian as mine.

Today my dreams are more humble as well. Days in education can be long, and many teachers are often overworked. However, our time is regularly filled with fascinating people, discussions, presentations, lectures, seminars, the many texts we read, and so on. Everything accumulates and creates a point for reflection. Design and/or art education is a context that lets you evolve. It seems to me also quite definite that the field of education makes you aware of the society you live in in more ways than you hope or expect. It doesn't let you stay too long in any comfortable corner, and although it can be distressing, I am also grateful for that. (Design) education is empowering.

*bell hooks, "Teaching to Transgress. Education as the Practice of Freedom", New York, Routledge, 1994, p. 19.

Dear Friend vol 34, February 2022. Written by Paul Soulellis, image by Robin Siimann, designed by Ott Kagovere, edited by Rachel Kinbar, concept by Sandra Nuut & Ott Kagovere, title font Cap Sizun by Eva Rank, text font Ladna Sans by Andree Paat (Kirjatehnika). Thank you Estonian Academy of Arts, Department of Graphic Design. Previous issues at gd.artun.ee/dearfriend

DEAR FRIEND,

LIBRARY QUEER SHARING SANCTUARY DOWNLOAD RISOGRAPH

I've been missing you. This morning I woke up before the sun, thinking about you. I knew that I had to write. I miss running into you. I miss meeting you for the first time, seeing you up close, walking beside you, catching up, hanging out, eating breakfast together, seeing your studio, meeting your friends, hearing your voice in the room. In the absence of these things, I listen, and do time travel. It's a way to keep going. I do it here in the library, finding things and bringing them into the present, so I've been thinking about how to share some of that with you. This letter is a small gesture, a gift, a signal, something to send out, something to do when bodies stay home, when we miss it all, and we wish for more.

June Jordan wrote about the library as *a sanctuary from the spectacle*. I found those words online and printed them out and put them here in the library, a small collection of zines and physical books and objects that we take care of at Queer. Archive.Work, across the street from Club Fantasies in Providence. Please come by and visit. We have Open Library Hours on Sundays, usually 12–3pm and the exact address is 400 Harris Avenue. The space changes every day, depending on who's here and what's happening. It's also a print and publishing studio, with Binch Press, so there's a lot of work going on too. It's a queer place for about 50 residents, members, and organizers, without many of the pressures that you'd expect in academia or traditional art world spaces, or even in some alternative art spaces. It's been such a sanctuary for us. Yes, it's *far from spectacle*, but it's not a hiding place. We gather, hang out, browse, read, write, and rest, in porous presence with each other. But we're also building something, support structures for living and working in crisis and thriving in community. We organize, learn, teach, practice, print, make, nourish, laugh together.

This is new work for me. I grew up in the US in the 70s and 80s, raised to believe in the individual, the empowered artist or designer or business person, the lonely figure of exceptional success. Trust no one, protect yourself, be ambitious, *rise to the top*. Ugh, I'm really trying to shift this now, from *me* to *we*. No rising, just reaching around and stretching with others. Things aren't going so well in the world, and we're not going to make it better with a land grab and a tiny house. Collective work is hard, but it's happening. I'm learning about communal power. I don't think there's any real way to do it except to do it. It's queer work, because each time we gather together without guarantees or predictable results or a hero leading the way forward, we push up against heteropatriarchy and refuse to play by those old rules.

Another thing we do in the library is publish. There's an SF9450 Risograph printer right there next to the shelves, a duplicator that I purchased a few years ago. We've got fluorescent pink, black, yellow, kelly green, burgundy, scarlet, purple, and aqua inks. It's connected to a computer so we can send PDFs to print but I really like to scan things directly on the flatbed. No InDesign, no grids, not much design at all, just using the riso printer as a camera that sees whatever I bring to the glass. It's such a beautiful machine, and I can use it to scan the library, one page at a time. This seeing-printer is how I made our most recent book, *resting reader*. I took all of its pages from our library shelves and printed 100 copies, and bound them on our Horizon BQ-140 perfect binder. The texts came together quickly while Omicron was spreading in December 2021. We had to stay isolated at a moment when I really wanted to engage, so I found ways to connect in the sanctuary. Gathered together in *resting reader* are these partners in time travel: Kendrick Daye, Kevin Quashie, Barbara Smith, June Jordan, 3rd World Gay Revolution, Dean Spade, The Care Collective, be oakley, Lin Marie Tonstad, adrienne maree brown, Thista Minai, Demian DinéYazhi', Alok Vaid-Menon, Sylvia Rivera, Dr. Erwin Lichtenegger and Dr. Lore Kutschera, The Spore Liberation Front, Eli Nixon, David Griffiths, noraa neither kaplan, Sara Ahmed, bell hooks & K Laster, Danielle Aubert, and the gay graphics collective. This book is some evidence of a moment, an ongoing moment. It's time travel because it contains the past, but it's about the future. Welcome to its future.

I decided to put "survival by sharing" on the cover of *resting reader*. It's a phrase I found in the QAW library in Danielle Aubert's book *The Detroit Printing Co-op* (2019), first used by Come!Unity Press, a "24-hour open access print shop run by a gay anarchist collective" in NYC in the 70s. I'm planning to visit their archives at NYU soon to see what else I can learn. We humbly revive their *survival by sharing* ethos now, fifty years later, in work like *resting reader* and in everything we do at the Binch/QAW studio. I sent 50 copies out in the mail, and the rest will be distributed here in person, when it's safe to do so.

I invite you to download a PDF version of *resting reader* right now, scanned from a printed copy. There's no real theme to this book, just some language that you may notice: rest, quiet, care, queer, sanctuary, reflection, collective, contamination, labor, joy, generosity. It's a reflective response to the *Urgency Readers* that we published over the last few years, and the focus on speed, crisis, and refusal in those volumes. The urgency isn't over and it didn't go anywhere; it's right here in this letter. But this reader comes after that. Take your time. I hope you enjoy it, and that we'll see each other very soon.

WITH YOU,
PAUL SOULELLIS

Dear Friend vol 35, March 2022. Written by Jack Self, image by Robin Siimann, designed by Ott Kagovere, edited by Rachel Kinbar, concept by Sandra Nuut & Ott Kagovere, title font Cap Sizun by Eva Rank, text font Ladna Sans by Andree Paat (Kirjatehnika). Thank you Estonian Academy of Arts, Department of Graphic Design. Previous issues at gd.artun.ee/dearfriend

CLOTHO FULCRUM AUGUST RIOTS POINT OF NO RETURN PUBLISHING

DEAR FRIEND,

The ancient Greeks thought about time and human narrative through the metaphor of a textile. Clotho (one of the three Fates) sat at her cosmic loom, before which stretched out an infinity of threads – each one representing a possible future. Clotho decided what would happen by plucking specific timelines, weaving them into the fabric of the present. As the textile stretched out behind her, it became history. Eventually, the cloth became worn and threadbare, until only tattered scraps remain.

There is one other important aspect to Clotho's task. Contemporary ideas about time (at least in the West) imagine that each individual is moving forward into the future, and leaving the past behind them. But Clotho is static. In this sense, the individual remains fixed in the present, and it is the future that comes to them, while the past is jettisoned.

The relevance of this metaphor is that I was recently asked to reflect on one of my first projects, a student publication at the Architectural Association called *Fulcrum* (2011–14). My relationship with time is not entirely like Clotho; I am unable to forget, which means that the tapestry of personal history never fades or falls apart. I sense the past as still going on. It is a place distanced from me by space, not by time. This is increasingly how others are experiencing the past, too. In the 1990s, for example, the 1980s felt like it was a very long time ago. This is because the only obvious material legacy was cars on the road, or some old street signs, the outdated style of a dentist's secretary (shoulder pads and a perm), and my parent's vinyls. Today, the 1990s feels contemporaneous with the present. A Google search makes no distinction between celebrity gossip that is 30 years old, or 3 days old – with the effect that it is possible to imagine the 1990s as a foreign country (inaccessible but real) and not a previous era.

For me, 2011 is still happening, as are all other years, months, days, hours, minutes and seconds. The challenge, when trying to communicate this experience to others, is how to capture the spirit of that time. What did it mean to live in 2011, and how was *Fulcrum* a reflection of that?

Fulcrum ran for 100 weekly issues, beginning the day Mubarak was deposed during the Arab Spring. After the 2008 crash, there was a tremendous spirit of hope for change. Obama's election campaign simply described the popular mood. But by 2010, it was clear that no change would come: Britain's government decided instead to punish the general populace with Austerity measures. I was at architecture school, and became increasingly active in the anti-cuts movements – large street protests by health workers, police and teachers against the reduction in budgets, closure of public libraries, increase in student fees, etc. All this eventually built up to the so-called August Riots (when anti-racism protests transformed into a week-long orgy of violence and theft; I saw buses set on fire in London, shops everywhere had their glass smashed, and parts of the city came under gang control). A few weeks after the Riots, the Occupy movement began. I found myself sleeping in a tent outside St. Paul's cathedral, mobilised into participatory democratic processes, and learning about self-organisation and anti-capitalist economics. I gave lectures at Occupy's Tent University on strategies of resistance in militarised urban settings.

I was living in poor-quality social housing at the time, and like most 23-year-olds I was angry and frustrated that the world was imperfect. The background desperation and anger in the United Kingdom mirrored my own mood. More likely, I have always been a straightforward product of whatever time and place I find myself in. The idea for *Fulcrum* was to create a publication that would try to capture the spirit of this moment and amplify it to a broader audience. The format was simple: since I didn't believe in an absolute model of truth, or the value of singular voices, there should always be two authors writing on the same topic. This was intended to show that there is always more than one way to think about a subject. A thick line divided the two articles. This line is the literal "fulcrum" (a thing that plays a central role in an activity) and the publication as a whole was trying to embody the other sense of "fulcrum" (tipping point, point of no return).

I graduated the week of the 100th issue, and I was very clear in the final editorial that the publication had ended. This was to highlight the fact that the publication as a whole constituted one project. It was also intended to encourage other, younger students to start their own publications (which they did; there were several that came directly afterwards).

Today, the possibility of goodbyes has been significantly diminished. We used to stand at the dock and wave to a departing steamer. We used to stand on the platform and wave to a departing train. Now, it is impossible to say goodbye. No sooner is a loved one out of sight than we are getting messages from them. But even psychologically, it is important to know when a project is finished, and so to have the strength to admit you must say goodbye.

Dear Friend vol 36, April 2022. Written by Claudia Doms, image by Laura Merendi, designed by Ott Kagovere, edited by Rachel Kinbar, concept by Sandra Nuut & Ott Kagovere, title font Cap Sizun by Eva Rank, text font Ladna Sans by Andree Paat (Kirjatehnika). Thank you Estonian Academy of Arts, Department of Graphic Design. Previous issues at gd.artun.ee/dearfriend

POLITICAL MORALISTIC GAME-CHANGING LUXURIOUS NON-SENSE

✱✱ DEAR FRIEND, A short note beforehand.

On March 3rd 2022, Sandra Nuut and Ott Kagovere invited me to write this letter. It was day 8 of the war, the Russian war against Ukraine. Today is day 28. Not a single day, not a single hour passes in which I do not think of the innocent people in Ukraine dying, fleeing, fighting for their country. Despite anything seeming meaningless in light of the war, I will try to phrase some thoughts about graphic design education, post-graduate life and ideas about the word 'political'.

Dear Friend, I don't remember your name; it's likely that I never knew. I don't remember your gender or appearance either, which is strange, because it is something that usually sticks easier than names. But I remember a question you asked me, and I have thought about it often since your visit. You asked me if my work was political.

I am no prophet writing that the word 'political' itself doesn't carry a moral value. Anything is political. It's interesting, though, that being political is associated with something positive in our Western academic context. It stands for progressiveness, voicing our values, initiating change. In Russia, where we met, the word is rather associated with terms like corruption, propaganda, fines, prison and other such negative connotations.

You came to Moscow in the summer of 2019 together with your fellow students and your teachers from Hamburg, despite the (already very bad) political situation in Russia. I showed you a compilation of video recorded interviews that I had conducted with my students, in which they talk about their education system, future prospects and their family circumstances. The differences to what we, as Western residents, are used to, are vast, as you will remember. At some point the conversation shifted, and you asked me about *my* work. You asked me if *my* work was political. I was confused and embarrassed at the same time. What was my work? Probably not the teaching and the interviews I had shown?

I pretended that I knew what was meant with the question, when in fact I didn't. I suddenly felt awkward because I didn't have a stack of artist books to show, or an exhibition I curated, or a range of cutting edge websites. Was I a graphic designer at all?

I quickly answered 'No'. A blurry explanation followed about how I started to find interest in unplanned details, the oddities of implemented designs, the discrepancies between the design and the execution and so on...

No matter how blurry the argument, it revealed to me my instilled belief about a political attitude having to be manifested in form. That in our profession criticality somehow needs to materialise in the design itself. Where did this perception of mine come from? I suspect from my education. In 2008 I graduated from the Rietveld Academie in Amsterdam—an experimental and free space that urged me to express my thoughts and opinions through my work. I was encouraged to do and say whatever I wanted, and I made good use of it. I left the academy with the impression that I had the potential to instill my beliefs in any project given to me. That I could, through the sheer force of my own will and unique talent, change the politics of life around me.

The reality couldn't have been removed further from this image. For many years I worked in London as a freelancer, designing for large corporations that did not care a dime for the well being of myself nor any other contributor in the long chain of production. Instead most of the time and money was invested in marketing, looming powerfully over all design decisions.

I can be terribly slow at understanding the world around me. As such it took me many years to rid myself of the presumption that graphic design contains within itself any moral or ethical guides that operate independently from its social or economic context. Graphic design is not moral, it is not ethical. It is a job.

It took me so long to understand this simple fact, that in my role as a teacher I continued to perpetuate the idea of a game-changing designer. I encouraged students to express their beliefs through their work and aim to become 'independent designers', never really defining what that would entail, especially for their financial future. Now I think that it is this combination which is completely nonsensical. There is no independence, no liberation without others. And I believe that education must stop promoting—directly or indirectly through their teaching staff, which will always function as a role model—the idea of the designer flying solo.

You must have graduated by now. Probably you know how hard it is to find interesting work for graphic designers. Work that means something to us, that we can identify with, that stimulates us intellectually and that is able to pay our bills.

Since I teach much less nowadays, and hence have less of a stable income, I was faced with making a decision about how to continue my design practice. I took the decision to work only with and for people whose agenda I identify with. I am allowed to do that because my partner pays most of the bills, so I am under no pressure to take on *any* job. I work for the local neighbourhood centre to announce movie screenings, I make brochures for political foundations, or lend my skills to otherwise social (and sometimes artistic) projects that I can stand behind. I made that decision, and I was able to make it because I had the privilege to do so. Any design that is not corporate is a luxury which most designers cannot afford, whether it is for economic reasons, sociopolitical ones or both.

Today I would still answer you that my work is not political. Not more than yoghurt packaging in the supermarket. I realised though that the politics of design are important to me, and that in order to find my place as a graphic designer, I need to stop thinking of myself as a graphic designer, but rather as a human being whose working life is formed by the social and economic forces around me.

Please write to me about your thoughts. I am terribly curious what your question was actually aimed at back then.

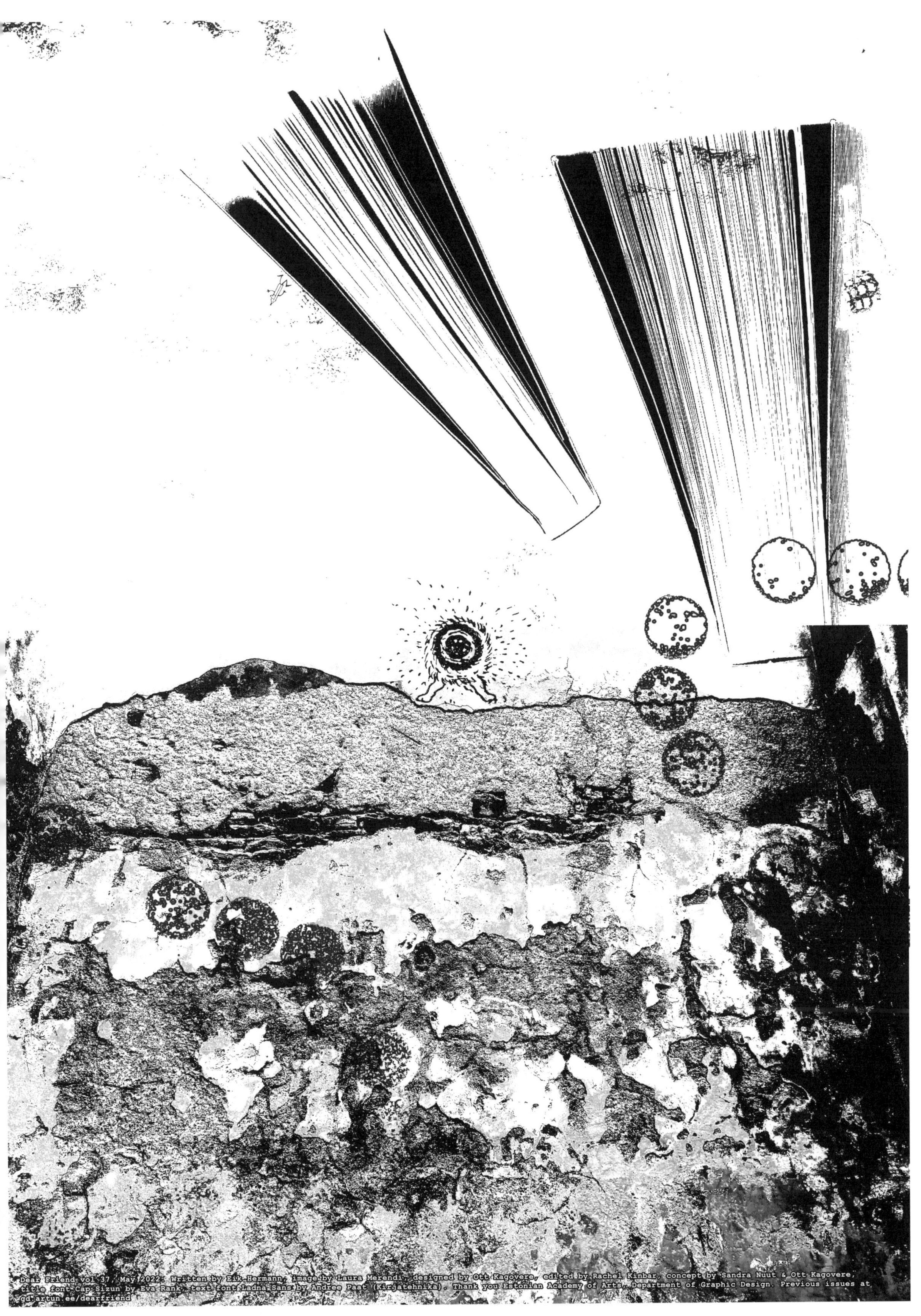

Dear Friend vol 37, May 2022. Written by Eik Hermann, image by Laura Merendi, designed by Ott Kagovere, edited by Rachel Kinbar, concept by Sandra Nuut & Ott Kagovere, title font Cap Sizun by Eva Rank, text font Ladna Sans by Andree Paat (Kirjatehnika). Thank you Estonian Academy of Arts, Department of Graphic Design. Previous issues at gd.artun.ee/dearfriend

ANTIHEROISM THOUGHTCRAFT WORKMANSHIP OF RISK DRAFTLAB HANDMIND

DEAR FRIEND,

How have you been? It's been ages since we last talked or even e-mailed. I really miss those conversations. As you know, I'm not too much into the small talk business and instead prefer the occasional very long and, ideally, intimate exchanges that start from nowhere and slowly acquire layers, exploring all kinds of nooks and niches, drawing you into this state of deep play. It's increasingly harder for me to find suitable "dialogue partners" or even occasions for such exchanges. Perhaps I haven't been really looking. Anyways, I just wanted to say I miss you.

While gathering thoughts about what to write to you, I've been thinking about what I've been up to these days. In contrast to the brutal events going around in nearby Ukraine, I'm having a hard time coming up with anything significant. Basically, I've just been typing a huge bunch of words on my computer.

Many of these words have gone into my upcoming Ph.D. thesis. It's still not very clear where it wants to go. I started with quite a specific plan, at least for my standards. And then it took off in a completely different direction. As you know, I'm a big fan of Witold Gombrowicz, who has wonderful pages about this. A writer starts writing a draft for his novel, and the first sentences happen to be in heroic tones. This compels him to add even more heroic sentences, fashion the plot in heroic lines, etc. Later, having published the novel, the writer can't bring himself to admit he'd just stumbled on this tone. So, he pretends he's a heroic *person*. Eventually, he doesn't even need to pretend.[1]

To be honest, this is what I dislike the most about writing: having to "defend your thoughts" and "own them" later. They're not really mine, are they? They're as much mine as a cat can be mine. Yet, I know people who still think this way—writing as an expression of oneself.

I'm increasingly treating thoughts as if they're materials. Not in the sense that they obey you and you shape them as you want. Being a master and all. For me, materials are defined by their particular ways of offering resistance and their particular wills or *tastes*, in the sense of what they agree or disagree with and what they are seeking or avoiding. Thoughts themselves *want* to go somewhere. You only have to listen. There's a lovely article by John Berger where he talks about negotiating with his sentences: they complain, you adjust them, they complain some more, until there is this murmur of approval.[2]

Craftspeople know all about the will of the materials. They also know a thing or two about hands. I mean, these things go hand-in-hand, don't they? In my thesis, I've been toying around with this idea of hands in the extended sense. If words and thoughts are materials, then I surely need hands to touch them, and by touching them, understand where they'll want to go.

I love how designer David Pye has written about it: doing something "by hand" has nothing to do with whether you use machines or not. The more relevant question is whether anything can go wrong in the process. If a lot can go wrong, we have what he calls workmanship of risk. If nothing can go wrong, it's workmanship of certainty.[3] Although my dentist mainly uses machines, she's certainly engaged in workmanship of risk. I'd like to hope the same could be said about me.

I don't remember if I ever told you that I used to take courses from the local massage school. Perhaps this is why it really pisses me off when people still oppose hands and minds. At its most basic level, massage is really easy, and everybody should know how to do it. But you sure have to *think-feel* all the time when giving a massage, and you have to *know* a lot—about bodies *and* souls—to do it really well. On the other side, good writing has the ability to touch you, and being engaged in it surely feels like a hands-on activity.

I'm tired of these stupid games of social status where it's always those who allegedly work with their minds who are more important than those who work with their hands. It's not only childish, but it also denies the hand-mind connection. This has been quite poisonous for our collective imagination, I think. Of course, the connection has always been there. People have always listened to their materials, their hands, but also to their environments and legs. They've had to. Most ideas reside exactly in those things, not in our heads. But it has been really hard to explore this connection consciously, as the high intellect *obviously* has no need for the lowly hands.

That's why I'm excited about the initiative we're preparing with my colleagues at the Estonian Academy of Arts—the Draftlab. The idea is to focus on the making processes of all kinds of disciplines, whether in arts, crafts, design, architecture, or theory and on the "scaffoldic" forms used for supporting those activities in their formative stages—sketches, prototypes, models, etc. The hope is to get some cross-pollination going on between the fields.

Looking back and reading what I've just written, I guess one phrase that stitches these themes together is dialogic open-endedness. While some writers have to know the last sentence of their novel before they can start writing, I need my writing to be open-ended—be more about opening and exploring things than about closing them, putting them in place. I hope to accomplish the same with my teaching: find ways of touching my students—not literally, of course, but also not only intellectually—in the hope of activating in them *their* materiality. But this open-endedness has to be dialogic in the sense that I also don't want to be "a slave to my materials," just blindly following where they want to go. My handmind should also have a say. Sometimes the materials have the upper hand, sometimes the handmind, with all sides playfully resisting and flirting with each other, giving rise to surprises. This is how I want to live.

How about you?

1. Witold Gombrowicz, Ferdydurke, Chapter 4.

2. John Berger, "Writing Is an Off-Shoot of Something Deeper."

3. David Pye, The Nature and Art of Workmanship, Chapter 2.

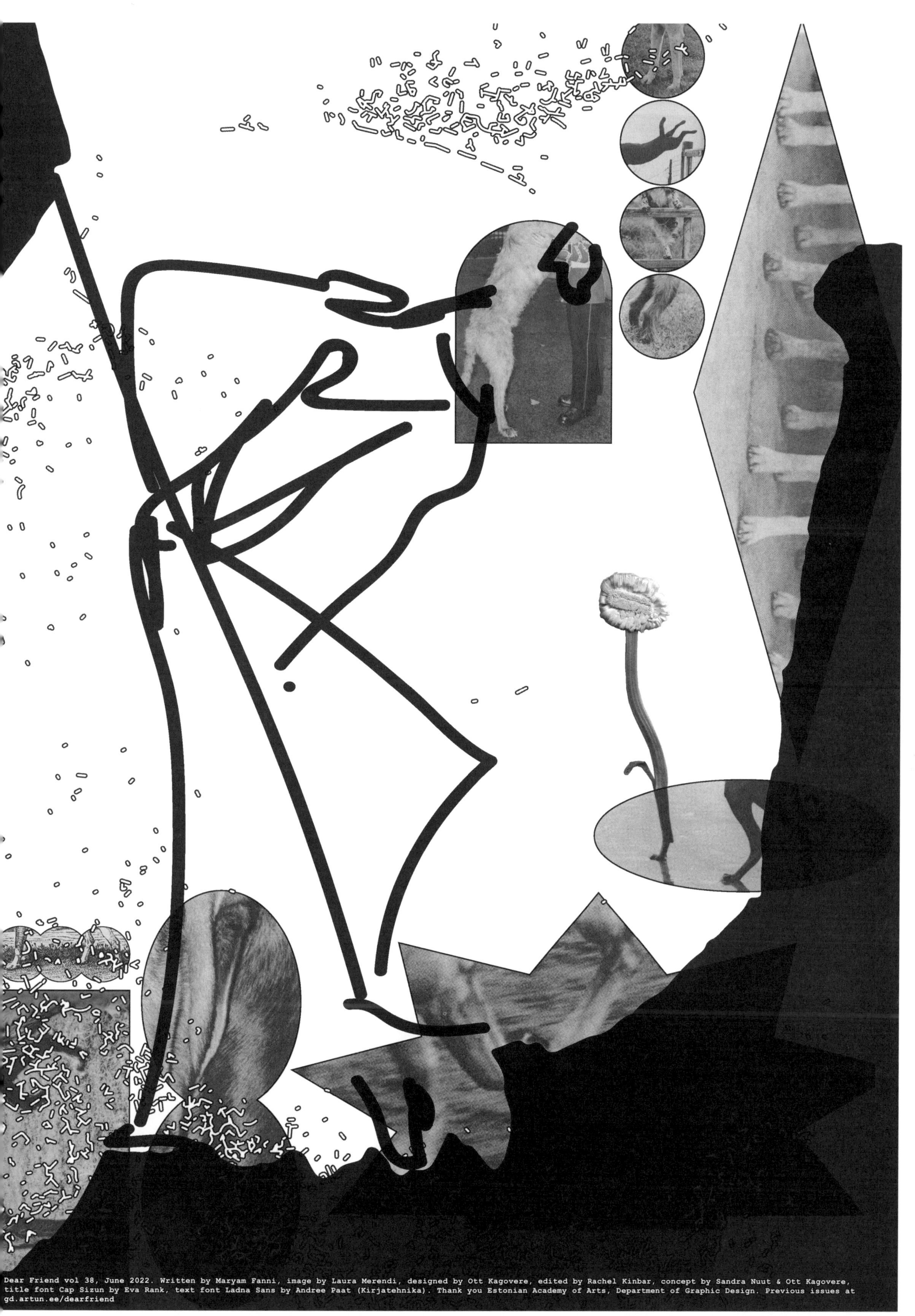

Dear Friend vol 38, June 2022. Written by Maryam Fanni, image by Laura Merendi, designed by Ott Kagovere, edited by Rachel Kinbar, concept by Sandra Nuut & Ott Kagovere, title font Cap Sizun by Eva Rank, text font Ladna Sans by Andree Paat (Kirjatehnika). Thank you Estonian Academy of Arts, Department of Graphic Design. Previous issues at gd.artun.ee/dearfriend

DIGGING REVOLUTIONARY TIME KINCAID PARIKKA LOCATION CLEANING

DEAR FRIEND,

Last weekend I went to the yearly share-out day of an allotment garden in a neighbouring suburb, excitedly hoping to be given the chance to take over a plot where I could grow potatoes, rhubarb, garlic, lots of marigold and perhaps some currant and raspberry bushes. Unsurprisingly, I wasn't the only one with this summer dream in mind after a never-ending Swedish winter—the queues for communal allotments have boomed during the pandemic and I returned home wishing for better luck next year. Most of the plots that were portioned out were quite overgrown and the woman guiding us kept repeating that one has to bear in mind that it is a time-consuming task to bring them into a good state. Back home, in addition to disappointment, I felt touched when thinking of the number of people who turned up that day and the bravery of taking on such challenge. Taking the responsibility of an allotment upon you means putting loads of effort without necessarily knowing the result.

A few years ago I was asked to help our local art exhibition space with their allotment as the staff were going on summer holiday and I lived nearby. It hadn't been cultivated for some years and thus needed to be prepared—lots of digging awaited—so I invited friends to join for a full-day activity and dig together. I can still summon the feeling of satisfaction as we, by late afternoon, had turned the soil up and down and were rewarded with the sight of a beautiful black square on the ground while sipping strawberry cordial from disposable cups. I have repeatedly returned to this memory to contemplate those hours of intense digging that we did together.

As opposed to a romantic idea of gardening that entails the lightness of harvesting and picking berries (walking at a slow pace, wearing a summer dress and straw hat), digging is intense, heavy and dirty. In the book about her garden, Jamaica Kincaid describes her digging self as "a picture of shame: a woman covered in dirt, smelling of manure, her hair flecked with white dust (powdered lime) . . . and her back crooked with pain from bending over".[1]

Digging is repetitive. Its monotony allows the mind to drift away and be in other places, while at the same time digging is literally an activity that deals with location. It is all about standing in place, and repeatedly turning to and processing the spot on which you are currently located. Digging is movement. But not a movement in space, like walking or running, not a movement forward, not linear. It is a circular movement, and in this regard it resembles cleaning.

Gender scientist Fanny Ambjörnsson[2] writes that cleaning is closely linked to time and time perception. The timeliness of cleaning points backwards, towards what we have left behind (the dirt), while society rewards what points forward, what is not stuck in an eternal scrubbing but rather promises "future", such as work trips and career-making. With reference to philosopher Fanny Söderbäck's concept of "revolutionary time"[3], Ambjörnsson suggests that the bodily experience in the act of cleaning allows for a new experience of time in which the past, present and future coincide. We clean as we have learned from previous generations, we are in the present when we struggle with the grease stain, but also in the future because we clean out of care for those who will soon walk on the clean and shiny floor. Similarly, I imagine that digging amalgamates the past (a long history of agriculture, burials, construction and so on), the present (the struggle of getting through the soil and picking up stones and rocks), and the future (preparing for plants, the coffin, or a house to be built).

Media theorist Jussi Parikka writes about digging as a methodological concept, arguing that not only is it a way of excavating and exploring beyond the surface, but it is also important to acknowledge the social dimension of digging, the verb, an activity that demands engagement. He draws from experiences and observations of hackathons and makerspaces as situations where collective digging takes place, in terms of people dedicated to getting across or through surfaces. The digging, he writes, "opens up visibilities and distributes a new sense of the infrastructural underground that underpins the surface of what we take for granted as a subject of everyday experience."[4] I myself have zero technical skills, but the DIY/DIT-culture is pumping in my veins. For me, equivalent situations would be fanzine workshops or public collage/cut-up workshops that my friends and I used to organize as a way of community crafting our local history beyond the urban renewal trajectories imposed on our neighbourhoods.

The more I think about it, I realize that much of what I have been up to the last decade has been different kinds of digging. All the times I have gathered with friends, colleagues, comrades, with a more or less vague or well-defined mission, a wish to "figure something out". Reading groups, research groups, activist groups or just undefined group constellations with a certain issue that brings the individuals together—formats and activities that have varied but one common denominator have been the search for an unknown, together.

I hope 2023 will bring me luck and award me an allotment where I can indulge myself in sweaty digging — you are of course invited to join (strawberry cordial will be served!). Until then, the diggings will take place in classrooms, by kitchen tables, by my desk and on my sofa, in culture and community houses, or wherever the diggings will take us.

MARYAM FANNI

1. Jamaica Kincaid, My Garden. Farrar,
2. Fanny Ambjörnsson, Tid att städa: om vardagsstädningens
3. Fanny Söderbäck, Revolutionary time: on time and difference
4. Jussi Parikka, "Digging" in Routledge Handbook of Interdisciplinary

Dear Friend vol 39, July 2022. Written by Indrek Sirkel, image by Pärtel Eelmere, designed by Ott Kagovere, edited by Rachel Kinbar, concept by Sandra Nuut & Ott Kagovere, title font Cap Sizun by Eva Rank, text font Ladna Sans by Andree Paat (Kirjatehnika). Thank you Estonian Academy of Arts, Department of Graphic Design. Previous issues at gd.artun.ee/dearfriend

FUTURE ME

PASSING TIME

REMEMBERING

SENSE OF TIME

TIME TRAVEL

PRESENT ME

✱✱ DEAR FRIEND,

One late evening a few weeks ago, I was watching another episode of Mindhunter on Netflix. I think it was one of the first episodes of the show, probably the second. Somewhere in the middle of the episode, the two protagonists—FBI agents Holden Ford and Bill Tench—are shown in a somewhat cliché montage of them traveling around the US for work and engaging in the most mundane of everyday activities: eating breakfast, drinking coffee, having a cigarette, driving a car, sleeping on an airplane, etc. This approximately two-minute scene is accompanied by the 1976 classic song *Fly Like An Eagle* by the Steve Miller Band. The intro lyrics have been playing in my head over and over again since that evening:

♫ Time keeps on slippin', slippin', slippin'
Into the future ♫

As you might have heard, I'm leaving my job at the Graphic Design Department of the Estonian Academy of Arts this summer. By the time you read this letter in July of 2022, I'll have been working here for exactly 15 years. I started in July of 2007 as one of the members of the BA admissions jury. I literally came directly from my own BA studies and even missed my graduation ceremony at the Gerrit Rietveld Academy in Amsterdam, as these two events coincided. During these past 15 years, I've worked as a teacher, associate professor, professor, and now for the last 6 years as the head of the department. I thought I was going to write this letter as a sort of goodbye to you. You know, to get all nostalgic and stuff. But to be honest, I haven't had any time to reminisce, not to mention the time to scribble anything down.

While consuming my daily dose of cooking videos on YouTube last week, among others I watched a clip by one of my favourite online cooking instructors: J. Kenji López-Alt. While masterfully sharing his recipe for a "really good beef stew" in his signature filming-with-a-GoPro-attached-to-his-head style, Kenji was contemplating the importance of the past, present and future in cooking. As an example, he suggests that if you want to be considerate to the future you, you might want to tie the bunch of thyme sprigs into a bundle before you throw them into the pot. Then the future you will be thankful that you don't have to fish out the sprigs one by one. At a certain point, he concludes on a philosophical note:

What I have found as I get older,
is that 'future me' becomes
'present me' much quicker than it used to.

On February 24, 2022, I was in Kärdla, Hiiumaa—the place where I spent all the summers of my childhood, up until I was 16 years old. Hiiumaa is the second biggest island of Estonia, North-West of the mainland, in the direction of Sweden. We were visiting the only living sister of my late grandmother Hilda, my grand-aunt Aino, who had her 91st birthday. She was in good spirits and healthy, still not wearing glasses. The same morning Russia had started the war in Ukraine. This clearly had an impact on everybody's mood in the room. Noticing this, Aino said that she'd seen enough war for one lifetime and started telling stories of our childhood when she and my grandmother were taking care of us kids during the summers. At some point she looked at me and asked:

Do you remember when you climbed
out of the window through the red rose bushes
to stay out late with the older kids?

Last year I designed and published a book for my good friend, the artist Paul Kuimet. He named the publication, his first monograph showing work from the last seven years, *Compositions with Passing Time*. The title comes loosely from one of the essays in the book by the writer Piret Karro. In the text, she analyses various ideas about time in Paul's oeuvre. She writes how Paul's looping 16mm films 'exacerbate the bafflement regarding the sense of time', how they 'depict a kind of fictitious space where time is stuck', and how the 'works rip open a new, personal dimension, one of subjective time flow'. And at a certain point in the essay she realises:

I could float in these space-times forever.

Since August of last year, I've had a copy of Jonas Mekas' *I Seem to Live. The New York Diaries VOL. 1. 1950–1969* on my studio table. Besides being a great book, it is also a lovely object—with its 824 pages, its spine measures more than five centimeters. Since I first got my hands on this publication last summer (in Vilnius, Lithuania, of all places!) I've been opening Mekas' diary now and then in random places and reading a few entries, most of which are noted with a specific date and year. It's a bit like time travel: page 235 takes you to July of 1960, flip a hundred pages forward and you're in February of 1963.

One day in the studio, probably while postponing doing some design work, I opened the book to page 789 which took me to February 3, 1969. February 3 is also my birthday, but not in 1969 as you know—I was born in 1984. On my birthday, 15 years prior to my birth, Jonas Mekas noted down the following:

This morning, walking crosstown, along 23rd Street,
I suddenly was stopped, I was stopped dead, by the
color of a small, red, tiny flower that I saw suddenly
before my eyes, and it was so very real, on a sunny hill,
and it was so red, so red. And I stood there, like an
idiot, remembering, a little red flower of my childhood, of
which even the name I have forgotten—but not its
color, its little leaves imprinted upon my eyes, upon my
memory. Then I recollected myself again, and
I continued walking.

Ok, it's getting late, I see the sun starting to set from my studio window in Tallinn. I'll head home; my dog Watson is probably waiting to go on our evening walk.

♫ Slippin' into the future, ♫

INDREK SIRKEL

Dear Friend vol 40, August 2022. Written by Maarja Kangro, image by Pärtel Eelmere, designed by Ott Kagovere, edited by Rachel Kinbar, concept by Sandra Nuut & Ott Kagovere, title font Cap Sizun by Eva Rank, text font Ladna by Andree Paat (Tüpokompanii). Thank you Estonian Academy of Arts, Department of Graphic Design. Previous issues at: gd.artun.ee/dearfriend

UKRAINE (IM)MORALITY OF IMPRESSIONS ADRENALINE SKELETONS SONTAG BAUDRILLARD

DEAR FRIEND,

Did you receive my postcard from Lviv? Sure, we must talk one of these days; sorry to have missed your Messenger call!

My postcard from Ukraine contained only some sardonic joking about how I didn't get killed; I sent it on the last day of my trip. When I think of the postcards you've sent me, the text on them is often very impressionistic: you describe the light, the colours and smells, tastes and sounds around you. Now, if I had to tell you about my journey in terms of sense perceptions and impressions, I would have to use a rather bright palette and, strange as it might seem, words that refer to pleasant sensations. The colour that I associate with my journey the most is bright green: quite obviously, as it was the end of April and the beginning of May, the time of golden light and bright green nature. Chestnuts were not in blossom yet.

As I crossed the Medyka–Shehyni border, my car trunk filled with boxes of tourniquets, elastic bandages and Israeli bandages for the Lviv volunteers, the sky was briefly overcast. Shehyni looked rather melancholy and shabby, although the golden church domes were shining as the sun came out again. But, hey, I was in Ukraine now! In the middle of wide-open green landscapes, driving on a road with strange deep holes in it, stopping occasionally to take photos of road signs wrapped in plastic (to mislead the enemy). It was 60 km to Lviv. Didn't I feel thrilled!

Sensations, perceptions, emotional responses, moods. It wouldn't make much sense to say that they are morally right or wrong. They just occur in our bodies and brains; who could claim that it's not correct to have adrenaline in your blood? No doubt, the thought patterns and ideological frameworks that shape our feelings can be held responsible, they can be interpreted as ethically sensitive or callous. And the way we express or withhold our responses can be judged. Ah, but this excitement! Thinking back to the day when I arrived in Ukraine at war, it appears to me as a cherished memory of spring light, greenness and warmth, and of the (yeah, dopaminergic!) expectation of experiences to come. There was the feeling of doing "the right thing" that writers don't get that often, do they? Just kidding.

I visited a couple of exhibitions in Lviv. One of them was in the Dzyga Art Centre, titled "The War Hour. Reflections..." which included 200 different works of art on the topic of war. It was an eclectic selection of caricatures and expressionist depictions of trauma. Spontaneously, I preferred the ones that were making harsh jokes about the Russian army and state, cheering people up for the fight. Yes, these absolutely unambiguous images made me happy: the Russian double-headed eagle being pushed into a meat mincer, or the statue of Diana from Lviv's Market Square carrying a FMG-148 Javelin, with the words, "The hunt on the orcs has begun." It wasn't as easy with the pictures that presented Ukraine as a victim. A Russian missile shattering pottery with Ukrainian patterns, for example. No, really, the belligerent images seemed to serve their purpose more. *The purpose*, indeed, while art cannot serve any other ultimate purpose than itself to function as art! Here we are again, back in what Jacques Rancière called the ethical regime of art: in this regime, art will provide images to bind together the ethos, and images are valued according to their utility. Don't you have the feeling that pure art, the ambivalence of meaning and openness to interpretations have somewhat eroded with the war? As well as the mode of being cool or épatant. It seems that these things can be fully restored only with the victory of Ukraine. Then, there is another phenomenon that has certainly increased during wartime, and that is the aura. Some of these works would have value just because they are *originally Ukrainian*.

One night, while I was comfortably in my hotel bed near the Opera, the photographer Dmitry Kotyuh sent me some photos. One was of a burnt human skeleton with its arms torn off in Makariv, near Kyiv. Who was this guy? Or was it a woman? I don't think I'm very good at discerning the sex of skeletons. If it was someone who defined their sex as "other", no medical expert would ever be able to detect it. It may have been a Russian soldier whose death will never be reported. Susan Sontag says that while narratives explain, photographs haunt. They do indeed. The skeletal guy keeps coming back to me. Touching the skin and flesh of my boyfriend, I find myself thinking about how that guy had his bare ribs spread out like a fan. All the soft tissue that had so much information stored in it, all the tissue that had once experienced the "thousand natural shocks that flesh is heir to" (sorry for this Shakespeare)—all this was irrevocably gone. Sontag also says that a photograph (of war) gives mixed signals. "Stop this, it urges. But it also exclaims, What a spectacle!" Was this one a spectacle? A remark able horror show? If it has its ghastly attraction, it's only because we will have to learn. That's the realm of destruction where some people's decisions and others' indecision will take us. It is here. You, yes, you too will have to do something if you don't want to end up like this.

Do you remember how, after the Gulf War, Baudrillard extravagantly said that the war didn't exist but was conjured up by the media? Later on, he talked about "war porn", as if the explicit images of atrocities in Iraq followed the aesthetics of porn. "Due to the prevailing rule of the world of making everything visible, the images, our present-day images, have become substantially pornographic." No such claim has been made about the images of the war in Ukraine. It's too close. Too real to speak of simulacra. The times have changed and Baudrillard is dead.

Well, now, I think we must talk to each other, or I'll get too serious.

Dear Friend vol 41, September 2022. Written by Neil Donkers, image by Pärtel Eelmere, designed by Ott Kagovere, edited by Rachel Kinbar, concept by Sandra Nuut & Ott Kagovere, title font Cap Sizun by Eva Rank, text font Ladna Sans by Andree Paat (Kirjatehnika). Thank you Estonian Academy of Arts, Department of Graphic Design. Previous issues at gd.artun.ee/dearfriend

STACKING DE APPEL CATCHING UP IN THE ARCHIVE BOOKS FIRE BURNT THINGS

DEAR FRIEND,

I've been stacking a lot lately. Lots of the same things.

With the archivists of de Appel and artist Mariana Lanari, we have placed an RFID tag in every book. Then we moved the entire archive 100 meters away to the exhibition hall of de Appel for the installation by Mariana Lanari—*Catching Up in the Archive*—last April and May.

The Archive of de Appel is composed of the library, the archive and the collection (unintended). It tells a multitude of stories about de Appel's living past and lively present through books, ephemera, video, audio, manuscripts, correspondence, witness reports and art.

The 16,000 books and periodicals were picked up and assessed at least three times, and in order to arrive at the final stacks in the exhibition, most of the books were also picked up a few times in between to be placed in an increasingly specific stack. And, after the exhibition, they were picked up and stacked a few times again to get them back to their usual placement in the cabinets in the archives of de Appel.

I am an archivist at heart.

Books, videos, photos, correspondence and everything else that is kept in the archive have their own placement per group, because the different materials have their own treatment and way of preservation. Climate, packaging and size influence this, but also the human way of organizing and retrieving. They all become different stacks of the same materials.

When nearly all 16,000 books and magazines were returned to their usual place in de Appel Archive, a bicycle battery exploded in my house. It wasn't too bad, a small fire that was quickly extinguished, but the whole house, everything was black with soot. "Worthless—in the dumpster," said the salvage expert. I decided to salvage things anyway so I wouldn't have to buy so many new ones.

I was standing in my black kitchen with stacks of black things on the counter and a stack of cookies on a cookie package caught my eye. One cookie is not a cookie, I thought. I've gone into overdrive over the past few years when it comes to gear and stuff. One wooden spoon is not a spoon. Five wooden spoons are an open-ended collection that grows by buying from thrift stores where an endless stream of things converge. Biscuits that are nicely placed in a stack in a silver foil sleeve are placed nicely next to each other, mechanically, but neatly stacked one by one.

So, the first stack were the jars and bottles with creams, shampoos, toothpaste, perfumes and detergents. Then the stacks with the soft stuff—towels for swimming, for the kitchen and bathroom, rugs, pillowcases and bed linen. Then stacks of little things made of reed and wood, baskets, boxes and spoons. Then stacks from the kitchen—plates, glasses, pans and cutlery. The stuff with solid surfaces I brought to the beach. Sand and salt are good polishing agents. The soot from the fire is a greasy emulsion and you have to apply a lot of pressure. It doesn't just come off. You really have to sand thoroughly.

Collections can always be rearranged and re-stacked. Two years ago, I invited artist/researcher Mariana Lanari to think along with me. I had made plans with designer Bert Kramer to make the entire archive of de Appel mobile. Travel to places, connect with other archives or collections instead of being a waiting body that stays in the same location and more or less presents itself in the same form.

Spaces-Run-Archive

One of the questions to Mariana was: whether we can implement RFID to minimize the size of the archive and give serendipity a helping hand. People often pull a book off the shelf that was next to the book they came to the archive for. I'm curious what happens when books no longer have a permanent place. And how that differs for the archivist and the user.

Still, I had to buy a lot of new things after the fire. You need certain things right away, like clothing, toothbrush, laptop, underwear, shoes. And while googling product photos, I noticed that products are increasingly being presented with more of the same, purchasable product in the photo. Especially things that serve to put other things in, to group, to store, to stack, and to make it discoverable, boxes, chests, containers, bags, drawers. Simply because the materials determine the way of storage. Photos and shoes need a different conservation than pans or works of art.

Mariana Lanari's project, *Catching Up in the Archive*, was a first stress test for Spaces-Run-Archive. For this work, Mariana, who desired a display of books that is not hidden behind a digital search bar, developed a technology application with Remco van Bladel (Archival Consciousness) intended for cultural libraries. Biblio-graph.org works as a tool to create a digital representation of fragments of physical collections. It is a community-sourced environment for data aggregation, mapping and visualization. Catching Up in the Archive was realized as an interactive installation in the exhibition space, a merely 100 meters from the archive space, where the entire archive was stacked horizontally. Without dividing them by substantive themes or alphabetically by name, the books went into neat stacks, sorted only by size. Each book was held and judged for size, color and shape. Neat stacks of books that have no made-up connection, except that they come from one collection presenting the history and story of de Appel. The visitors wandered among the stacks, their eyes wandered over the stacks and they made their own choices and connections, rearranging the stacks again and again.

The archivist in me experienced some tense moments. In the archive I know roughly where a book is, but in this sea of book stacks.....? When people asked for a specific book, I could find it by wandering through and letting my eyes scan, which was surprising. I thought I could only locate books because I knew where they were on the shelves, but apparently size, shape, design and color are also stacked somewhere in my brain.

For now, I'm wandering and looking around my black house, seeing what can be salvaged and grouping, stacking and enclosing my things as if in the archive.

I am an archivist at heart.

PS: Only charge batteries when you are present and awake!

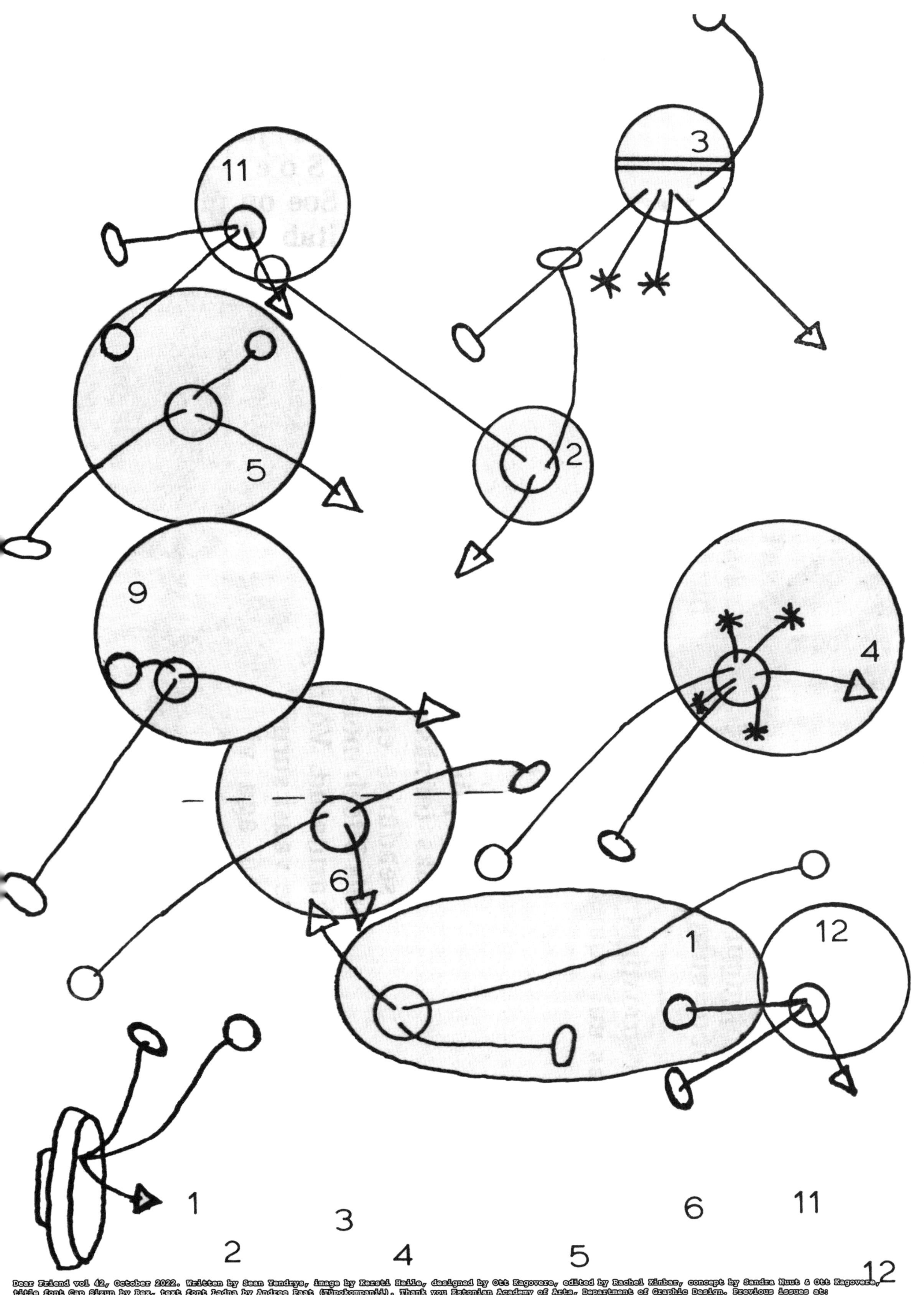

Dear Friend vol 42, October 2022. Written by Sean Yendrys, image by Kersti Heile, designed by Ott Kagovere, edited by Rachel Kinbar, concept by Sandra Nuut & Ott Kagovere, title font Cap Sizun by Rex, text font Ladna by Andree Paat (Tüpokompanii). Thank you Estonian Academy of Arts, Department of Graphic Design. Previous issues at: gd.artun.ee/dearfriend

DEAR FRIEND,

Last year I hung out with a friend who I hadn't seen for a long time. We caught up by spending an afternoon taking a walk around Gleisdreieck park. As inevitably happens when two people who work too much in the cultural field meet, the conversation eventually turned to practice. We were expressing how tired we felt from juggling too much too fast, how it hurt the quality of the work we did, and how poor our work/life balance was. I wondered if there was ever going to be a moment when things might become manageable.

She told me that she recently realised she's a slow maker, and how important it's been for her to find ways of supporting it. If someone wants to work with her, they need to understand this before she can agree to collaborate. That means either inviting her earlier into a process, or giving her the time she needs to do the very good and thoughtful work she knows she would do. This resonated so much for me. I'm also a slow maker, and a slow learner, too. It takes a lot of time for me to do things well, and in a way that feels good for me, but rarely do I put myself in a position that acknowledges it, often leading to the very anxieties we discussed.

This morning I was reading from *The Undercurrents* by Kirsty Bell. In it she coincidentally spends a few pages writing about having once lived in front of Gleisdreieck, and the developments which led to it being the park it is now. Sometimes I think I might have too many books, at least for my pace of reading. But I like being able to pull one off the shelf and sit with it, reading only from a few pages or maybe a whole chapter, before putting it back. I might pick it up again later that day, or the next, or even a year from now—choosing instead to spend time with other books, also in a similar manner. It's not the most productive way to finish a book, but I have trouble holding attention, and I'm likely to miss what I'm reading if I go for too long with it.

A few years after finishing school, I started to miss the feeling of checking in with a classmate at their desk, sharing what we were up to in the hours outside of class. These felt like the moments where I learned the most. This led me to organising a series of small and informal talks from the living room of my apartment. At first we had an audience of five (including my two very accommodating roommates), but sometimes welcomed as many as 30 guests, some needing to stand out in the hallway. One of my favourites was a talk by Eliot Gisel and Nina Paim, sharing the first steps of research they were doing for an upcoming essay on school uniforms. It was scheduled on a busy evening, so only around six people came, but we still decided to squeeze together, all on one couch—some leaning over from behind—surrounding Nina's laptop as they showed us the bits and pieces they had gathered.

Now that I work as head of the new MA in graphic design at the Estonian Academy of Arts, we've been trying to find ways of bringing a similar spirit into the program. It hasn't been the easiest—there's so much of the institution that still needs navigating—but I think we've started to find a balance between the formal and informal. Spending an evening cooking dinner together when a guest teacher visits has been a nice tradition so far. Another has been to organise a week-long residency for graduating students, in support of their thesis process—always hosted by a current student in their home country (Latvia and Iceland, so far). This gives everyone a chance to spend a week together, cooking meals, going for walks, and using the time to more slowly discuss the development of everyone's work away from the school, in a setting arranged by the students.

That reminds me, I just returned from a short trip to see *documenta fifteen* in Kassel. It's the mega-mega of the mega-art events, and one that traditionally takes itself very seriously. I'm normally suspicious of something so big, but also can't help but be curious about what happens when given the time and resources to make something at such a massive scale. This edition felt different though, it was under the direction of ruangrupa, a collective from Jakarta, who came with a decentralised approach—inviting a diverse group of collectives, who themselves were responsible for inviting more collectives, and so on, until over 1,500 artists were included.

There was an energy throughout the city, with many of the artists still present even weeks after the opening. That's because many spaces were less concerned about physical artefacts and more about supporting conditions for gathering, and spending time to share resources, services and knowledge. This included artists organising a communal kitchen and garden as a public meeting space, a full scale printing press to produce books for other artists, and even operating a daycare centre open everyday for the duration of the event. I had the sense that if you were to visit in July and later again in September that you might get a totally different experience from the last. While reading the exhibition guide, I found the curators describing this intention as *nongkrong*, an Indonesian slang term for "hanging out together."

What I like about hanging out is how flexible it is to facilitating different levels of engagement. It doesn't necessarily demand any one thing, but can support many things at once. It might end in a place completely different from where it started. Who and what is guiding might also change, and you can choose to be an active part in that or spend your time listening. It can be deeply intimate, or free for anyone to take part. You can come in for just a moment, spend hours highly involved, or continue to dip in and out as you please. It reminds me that what I like most about being a graphic designer is similar to being a good host: it's a way of inviting people into something, and letting them spend time with it at their own speed.

Dear Friend vol 43, November 2022. Written by Rachel Kinbar, image by Kersti Heile, designed by Ott Kagovere, edited by Rachel Kinbar, concept by Sandra Nuut & Ott Kagovere, title font Cap Sizun by Rex, text font Ladna Sans by Andree Paat (Kirjatehnika). Thank you Estonian Academy of Arts, Department of Graphic Design. Previous issues at gd.artun.ee/dearfriend

LANGUAGE · LIBERATION · JOY · ABOLITION · EDITING · PEOPLE

DEAR FRIEND,

Sometimes when I read or hear something so true, I feel an expansion of my consciousness that moves me to tears. Has that ever happened to you? For example, when I first read this quote, every cell in my body said YES:

"No one who has ever touched liberation could possibly want anything other than liberation for everyone."
—Rev. angel Kyodo williams

As a white, able-bodied, cis-het-presenting person, there's a lot of systemic bullshit I don't have to deal with or can get around with relative ease. I know this. You know this. *And* I spent years living under very difficult circumstances beyond my control. I know the joy of liberation, of freedom, that undeniable lightness of being. Mine was a small, personal liberation, and in the words of the great Fannie Lou Hamer: "Nobody's free until everybody's free."

Abolition isn't only about abolishing slavery or prisons. I am specifically referring to the movement that aims to tear down harmful institutions that oppress the poor and disabled and queer and people of color and instead build healthy systems of safety and accountability in their place. The people impacted are not "others"—they are me, my friends, my family, my community. Abolition is a practice, a way of being and living. It is a choice, a million choices in succession. It is reaching for joy and wholeness in all that we do.

This letter seems heavy, but I don't *feel* heavy. It annoys me that seriousness and playfulness are considered opposites. Why can't something be delightful *and* significant? I'd argue that the people dancing and twerking at protests are making some of the most profound statements, and they're having fun and spreading joy while doing it. As the copyeditor of *Dear Friend*, I've really enjoyed engaging with every letter. Some letters led me down internet rabbit holes, some made me laugh or think about something new, some led me to the authors' websites or Instagram accounts. Having language to share ideas and express ourselves in this way is a spectacular miracle!

The slow elongation of the human throat, tongue, and larynx 50,000 years ago made speech possible, and 5,500 years ago humans began to make the transition from orality to literacy. There are studies that show how languages are shaped by their local geography and environment. Another study shows that our personalities shift when we switch languages. Other research shows how language influences how we think. The architecture of this co-evolution, co-design of language, place, and body astounds me. At the same time, I am aware that language—and the English language in particular—has been used as a genocidal weapon to eradicate culture and history—of enslaved people, of Indigenous peoples, of immigrants. What happens when a language leaves its homeland and invades the mouths of others? I think the violence of it changes all of us.

After editing Alicia Olushola Ajayi's letter in 2020, I sent this note to Sandra and Ott:

Maybe I shouldn't admit this, but other than for texts intended for scholarly journals, I have pretty much abandoned using editing manuals like the Chicago Manual of Style or the Oxford Style Manual. I've been writing and editing for 20 or so years, and I have slowly moved away from the concept of "correct" or "prefect" English because it is so tied to elitism and is used as a tool of white supremacy. As I see it, my role as a copyeditor is to preserve the voice and message of the author and ensure that their ideas are communicated clearly. Many people think copyediting is just technical work. Technical knowledge comes into play, for sure, but there are many discretionary decisions made while editing.

My move away from gatekeeping "proper English" and from rules that limit and inhibit meaning is part of my abolitionist practice, as are examining how I parent my child, how I hold myself and others accountable, how I organize in my community, how I earn, spend, and share money, how I dance, how I make art, how I build relationships, *how I do anything*. Abolition brings freedom, and I've tasted that joy, that liberation, that abundance, that love. And how could I not want that for you? For all of us?

XO,
RACHEL KINBAR

1. I don't want to go into it again now, but I'll never forget how, when I first told you, that you

2. https://www.nature.com/articles/

3. https://academic.oup.com/jcr/article-abstract/

4. Check out 7,000 *Universes: How the Language We*

Dear Friend vol 44, December 2022. Written by Ott Kagovere, image by Kersti Heile, designed by Ott Kagovere, edited by Rachel Kinbar, concept by Sandra Nuut & Ott Kagovere, title font Cap Sizun by Rex, text font Ladna Sans by Andree Paat (Kirjatehnika). Thank you Estonian Academy of Arts, Department of Graphic Design. Previous issues at gd.artun.ee/dearfriend

OSWALD TSCHIRTNER

IMPROVISATION IN GRAPHIC DESIGN & MUSIC

ANTOINE BEUGER

✱✱ DEAR FRIEND,

I am not sure if you remember, but when we first met a few years ago in a busy bar, we bonded over our mutual interest in contemporary classical music. We were both graphic designers, so naturally the conversation flapped between design and music. At some point I blurted out a concern of mine—*don't you think it's strange that improvisation, so common and natural in music, seems to lack an equivalent in graphic design?* Immediately after, I felt silly for saying it. Of course there is improvisation in graphic design! There must be? My nervous inner monologue took over, but your response was calming. You told me that you have been dealing with this throughout your whole career. We talked about it for a long time but were never able to exhaust the topic. What is improvisation in graphic design? What is improvisation in general? There are too many answers, too many nuances to take into consideration.

In improvised music, I am not interested (at least at the moment) in free form, out of the blue, spontaneous expression, but rather in *composition* as a condition of improvisation. Perhaps this sounds counter intuitive? After all, composition and improvisation seem to be in the opposite corners of musical expression, but let me explain further. A composition of that kind is written so that it leaves room for other people besides the Composer. The composer proposes a score with empty blanks, and the musicians (sometimes even the audience members) are meant to fill them in. These blanks are demarcated by a set of conditions and together they form a space that invites or perhaps even demands improvisatory (musical) gestures. This approach takes into consideration the fact that a piece is not complete without a collective—the musicians and the audience. It does not see music as an abstract, almost platonic idea, but as something that happens in a certain place at a certain time and is possible only when it is actually played and heard. To some, this might seem radical or strange, but in my opinion it is the most realistic view on music. Everything else seems to be an idealization.

There are many examples of this approach, but the musical piece "Tschirtner[1] Tunings for Twelve" by Antoine Beuger[2] is a good example. The score is a collection of 30 pages from which the players themselves can choose any number of pages to play. Each player has only one or two tones assigned for each page and they can choose any octave or tuning for the given pitches, as well as when to play them. The dynamics are soft throughout and the duration of the piece is meant to be long or very long. That's the score—as open as a door.

When played, the piece feels strange and empty. Perhaps unfinished? Without a clear ending or an overarching theme. Like Tschirtners drawings, they exist without telling us why. They make us think about the art or the music itself, not something secondary, like a plot or a moral conclusion.

The piece is also interesting because it is an event, not an abstract construction. The composer cannot pre-listen to it in his "mind's eye". The composer becomes a member of the audience, because the actual realization of the piece is as much a surprise for them as it is for anybody else. An approach like this seems very clear, but why was it so hard to find an equivalent of this in graphic design?

Looking back at my thinking, I find several misconceptions. I always thought of the designer as the composer, whereas recently I have come to realize that the designer's work is much closer to the interpreter or the musician. A client comes to me with a score (a brief) and my job is to make sense of it and propose an interpretation. Sometimes the score is very loose. Just a few ideas, associations, a couple of texts, a deadline. Other times it's very fixed. Occasionally the composer (the client) knows exactly what, how and when they want it, and all they ask of me is to play along. At times the composer drops off the score like a burden. They can't bear it any longer. There is too much stuff. They need someone to make sense of it, someone to have a conversation about it.

When thinking of the designer as a composer, I was too fixated on myself and my creation. Whether I wanted it or not, it became the lonely road of the solitary genius trying to create *ex-nihilo*. But when thinking of design work in terms of interpretation, it becomes a dialogical endeavour and only partially reliant on me.

Another misconception is thinking of design as something abstract. Perhaps even something finished and under control. A much more realistic way of seeing design is to think of it as an event. In that sense a musical event, like a concert, and a graphic event, like publishing a series of letters over a period of four years, are very similar.

A friend of mine told me that she does not understand the publishing schedule of *Dear Friend*. The letters seem to arrive at erratic intervals. This comment amused me a great deal because for me the publishing schedule has been the clearest thing about the endeavour—one letter each month! But of course this is an abstraction. In reality, it gets stretched out and the most surprising publishing rhythms will occur. Sometimes the letter comes in the beginning of the month, sometimes in the end, sometimes we are a little late and it comes in the beginning of the next month, and then it might happen that you get two letters within the same month. Or you get none because they get lost in the mail—anything is possible. But even if the publishing schedule is somewhat flexible, the important thing is that whether you expect it or not the letter will eventually arrive.

This realization has made me see *Dear Friend* as an extremely long graphic event. The event spans four years. Similarly to the *Tschirtner Tunings,* it has a partially fixed score: a fixed format, a fixed folding system, and a fixed colour scheme. The tempo is slow or very slow, not fast or immediate (like daily news or social media) and its tone is undemanding—you can read it if you want to. If not, no harm done.

I am relieved to say that after all these years, I finally understand what you meant. I too have been dealing with improvisation throughout my whole career. I always have. I just wasn't aware of it.

OTT KAGOVERE

2 Antoie Beuger (b 1955) is a Dutch composer and founder of the Wadelweiser group.

1 Oswald Tschirtner (1920-2007) was an Austrian artist who spent most of his life in mental institutions. His drawings are very minimal, sketch-like, mostly line-based depictions of people. I recommend looking them up; they are breathtaking!

ALICIA AJAYI
is an architectural designer, researcher, writer, and (trying to figure it out) based in NYC. Dear Friend 16 aliciaoajayi.com

MAI BAUVALD
is an artist and graphic designer based in Tallinn and Amsterdam. They are currently exploring the phenomenology of bodies and the mundane. Dear Friend 22, 23, 24

STUART BERTOLOTTI-BAILEY
is a British graphic designer, writer and editor, founder of the journal Dot Dot Dot and it's successors Bulletins of the Serving Library and The Serving Library Annual. Dear Friend 28 servinglibrary.org

CLAUDIA DOMS
is a graphic designer and teacher living in Leipzig, Germany. Dear Friend 36 claudiadoms.com

NELL DONKERS
has managed the archive (library, archive and collection) of De Appel in Amsterdam since 2002 and made it digitally and physically accessible. Dear Friend 41

PÄRTEL EELMERE
is a graphic designer and illustrator who would like to see less trees cut down. Dear Friend 39, 40, 41

MAARIN EKTERMANN
is working on intersections between contemporary art and more-or-less experimental education. Dear Friend 24 proloogkool.eu/en

ROSEN EVELEIGH
is a designer, writer and researcher working independently or with artists, archives, editors, cultural institutions and publishers to produce graphic identities, typefaces, websites, texts, talks, books and other works. They are interested in the historic and methodological relationship between graphic design and queer culture. Dear Friend 26 roseneveleigh.com

MARYAM FANNI
is a graphic designer based in Stockholm and Gothenburg, Sweden, a PhD student in Design at HDK-Valand Academy of Art and Design, University of Gothenburg and co-founder and member of collectives MMS, SIFAV and Mapping the Unjust City. Dear Friend 38 maryamfanni.se

MARTINA GOFMAN
is an illustrator working in the field of graphic design and makeup. Her works vary from creating unworldly characters with prothetics to designing websites with decorative twists. Dear Friend 31, 32

SAARA HANNUS
is an artist and curator working in the intersections of sexual/romantic relationships and art making. Dear Friend 31 saarahannuslove.tumblr.com

KERSTI HEILE
is a graphic designer based in Tallinn, Estonia. After graduating from Estonian Academy of Arts, she worked as a freelance designer mainly in the cultural sector. Since Spring 2022, she works in the design studio AKU in Tallinn. Dear Friend 42, 43, 44 kerstiheile.com

EIK HERMANN
is a philosopher and a teacher working in close collaboration with architects. Dear Friend 37

PAUL JOHN
is an artist who works in abstract photography and publishing, currently he is the coordinator of Printing and Publishing at the Jan van Eyck Academie. Working at the intersection of printmaking and institution building Paul John is the co-founder of both Brooklyn Art Book Fair and Endless Editions, based out of the Robert Blackburn Printmaking Workshop in New York City. He now serves as an advisor and volunteer at both organizations. Dear Friend 18 endlesseditions.com bkabf.info thinkingaboutmyfavoritetree.com

MARIA JUUR
aka Maria Minerva is an Estonian producer and activist based in Los Angeles. Dear Friend 17 mariaminerva.com

OTT KAGOVERE
is a Tallinn-based graphic designer and a teacher in the Department of Graphic Design at the Estonian Academy of Arts. Dear Friend 10, 21, 32, 44 ottkagovere.com

MAARJA KANGRO
is a writer, translator and librettist based in Tallinn. Dear Friend 40

ARJA KARHUMAA
is a text designer, a feral academic, and a language animal. She is Assistant Professor and Head of Programme in Visual Communication Design (vcd.aalto.fi) at Aalto University ARTS, Finland. Dear Friend 25 people.aalto.fi/arja.karhumaa

KRISTINA KETOLA BORE
is assistant curator at Kunsthall Stavanger, writer, and all-round lover of Estonian bread. Dear Friend 2 kristinaketola.work

NICOLE KILLIAN
is an artist and design educator living and working in Richmond, Virginia. Dear Friend 6 nylondip.com

RACHEL KINBAR
is exploring what it means to be human as a community and mutual aid organizer, writer, editor, gardener, artist, parent, and partner. Also: half of noise/poetry duo Unfade, co-editor of Bonk! Magazine, and copyeditor of Dear Friend. Dear Friend 43

TUOMAS KORTTEINEN
is a graphic designer and visiting tutor at the Visual communication design programme at Aalto University, Finland. Dear Friend 19 tuomaskortteinen.tumblr.com

KEIU KRIKMANN
is a writer, translator and curator based in Tallinn. Dear Friend 11 keiukrikmann.com

ANNELI KRIPSAAR
is a designer and front-end developer based in Tallinn, Estonia. Dear Friend web-archive

KADRI LAAS
is a cultural manager, the director of operations at Kai Art Center and the project manager at Estonian Contemporary Art Development Center. In 2016–2019, Laas was the managing director of the Tallinn Photomonth contemporary art biennial. Dear Friend 9

ELSE LAGERSPETZ
is a creative worker based in Tallinn, Estonia. She holds an MA degree in Visual Cultures, Curating and Contemporary Art from Aalto University, Finland, and currently works at the Department of Graphic Design at the Estonian Academy of Arts. Alongside educational and graphic design activities Lagerspetz works with texts, writing and translating for publications and exhibitions, and together with Loore Viires runs the loose-format publishing project Knock! Knock! Books. Dear Friend 3 knock-knock.ee

LIEVEN LAHAYE
is an artist and librarian, he publishes 'Catalog', a serial publication on cataloging. Dear Friend 4 cataloging.xyz

JAMES LANGDON
is an independent graphic designer, writer and professor in communication design at the Hochschule für Gestaltung in Karlsruhe. Since 2004, he has worked closely with many artists designing publications and exhibitions. Dear Friend 14 jameslangdon.net

JUNGMYUNG LEE
is a graphic and type designer based in Amsterdam, from where she runs the independent type foundry J-LTF (Jung-Lee Type Foundry). Dear Friend 12 jung-lee.nl

KAI LOBJAKAS
is a design historian and the director of Estonian Museum of Applied Art and Design. Dear Friend 27

LAURA MERENDI
is making sure that graphic design students at Estonian Academy of Arts have enough paper and is also, when there's time, a graphic designer. Dear Friend 36, 37, 38

MICHELLE MILLAR FISHER
is currently the Ronald C. and Anita L. Wornick Curator of Contemporary Decorative Arts at the Museum of Fine Arts, Boston. Her work focuses on the intersections of people, power, and the material world. Dear Friend 30 michellemillarfisher.com

MARIA MUUK
is a designer and writer based in Tallinn. After completing the Critical Studies MA programme at the Sandberg Institute in Amsterdam in 2019 and working as a pastry chef for half a year, she is now again excited about design and its history. Dear Friend 8 mariamuuk.ee

SHEERE NG
is a writer and researcher living in Singapore. Her work focuses on the intersections of food, identity and immigration. She is also part of the writing studio In Plain Words. Dear Friend 23 sheere-ng.com

SANDRA NUUT's
work includes writing, lecturing and curatorial projects in the design field. She is a curator at the Estonian Museum of Applied Art and Design. Previously she worked at the Estonian Academy of Arts and New York-based gallery Chamber. Dear Friend 1, 13, 22, 33 sandranuut.com

MIKK OJA
is a graphic designer and writer based in South Estonia. Dear Friend 25, 26, 27

ANDREE PAAT
is a freelance graphic and type designer based in Tallinn. He is a one of the co-founders of the type design studio Tüpokompanii together with Aimur Takk.

LAURA PAPPA
is a graphic designer based in Amsterdam active mainly in the cultural field. Dear Friend 15 laurapappa.biz

REX
is an artist, filmmaker and web developer. They are based in the Netherlands where they enjoy riding motorcycles and petting cows. Dear Friend 28, Dear Friend 29 J2nku.club

JOHANNA RUUKHOLM
is a graphic designer and artist. Her graphic works vary from websites to illustrated visuals, which often come to life as ceramic installations. Dear Friend 30, 32

JACK SELF
is an architect based in London. He is Director of REAL foundation and Editor-in-Chief of Real Review. Dear Friend 35 jackself.com

INDREK SIRKEL
is a graphic designer, educator, and publisher based in Tallinn. Since 2007 he's worked at the Estonian Academy of Arts (EKA). Together with Anu Vahtra, he is the founder of Lugemik Publishing (2010) and Bookshop (2013). Dear Friend 39 lugemik.ee

ROBIN SIIMANN
is a graphic designer based in Tallinn. Dear Friend 13, 33, 34, 35

PAUL SOULELLIS
is an artist and educator based in Providence, RI. His practice includes teaching, writing, and experimental publishing, with a focus on queer methodologies and network culture. Dear Friend 34 soulellis.com

TRIIN TAMM
produces books, objects, collections, and confusion—outside of a linear progression, and without succumbing to the constraining expectations of the art system. Dear Friend 7

LAURA TOOTS
is a cultural worker based in Tallinn. Toots received an MA degree in Fine Arts from the Estonian Academy of Arts (2011). Toots is interested in different collective working practices and experiences. She has organised projects large and small—from publications to art biennials—aiming to bring together different professionals for a wider exchange of ideas. Dear Friend 9

ALICE TWEMLOW
is a researcher interested in design's complex inter-relations with time and the environment. Her research manifests in writing, exhibitions, conferences, and education. Dear Friend 29 alicetwemlow.com

LOORE VIIRES
is a graphic designer and publisher at Knock! Knock! Books, currently in-between studies and projects. Dear Friend 20 knock-knock.ee

SEAN YENDRYS
is a graphic designer based in Berlin, and teacher at the Estonian Academy of Arts. Dear Friend 42 seanyendrys.com

JUSTIN ZHUANG
is a Singapore-based writer and researcher who sees the world as designed, and not designer. Dear Friend 5 justinzhuang.com